THE *Spirituality* OF **BREAD**

DONNA SINCLAIR

THE *Spirituality* OF BREAD

Northstone

Concept: Northstone Team
Editor: Mike Schwartzentruber
Cover: Verena Velten and Margaret Kyle
Interior design: Verena Velten and Margaret Kyle
Proofreading: Dianne Greenslade
Photo credits: see page 158

Northstone is an imprint of **Wood Lake Publishing, Inc.** Wood Lake
Publishing acknowledges the financial support of the Government of
Canada, through the Book Publishing Industry Development Program
(BPIDP) for its publishing activities.

BNC CERTIFIED | BIBLIOGRAPHIC DATA 2006-07

At Wood Lake Publishing, we practice what we publish, being guided by
a concern for fairness, justice, and equal opportunity in all of our relationships with employees and customers. Wood Lake Publishing is an employee-
owned company, committed to caring for the environment and all creation.
Wood Lake Publishing recycles, reuses, and encourages readers to do the
same. Resources are printed on 100% post-consumer recycled paper and
more environmentally friendly groundwood papers (newsprint), whenever
possible. A percentage of all profit is donated to charitable organizations.

Library and Archives Canada Cataloguing in Publication
Sinclair, Donna, 1943-
        The spirituality of bread / Donna Sinclair.
Includes bibliographical references.
ISBN 978-1-896836-85-0
1. Bread. 2. Bread--Religious aspects--Christianity. 3. Cookery (Bread).
I. Title.
TX769.S52 2007   641.8'15   C2007-900274-9

Published by Northstone
9590 Jim Bailey Road, Kelowna, BC V4V 1R2 Canada
www.northstone.com
250.766.2778

Printing 10 9 8 7 6 5 4 3 2 1
Printed in Hong Kong

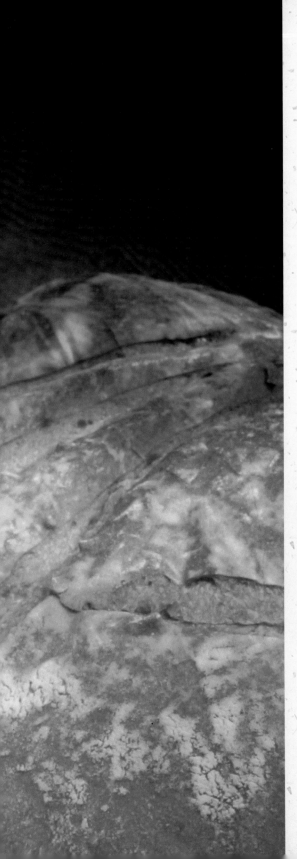

Contents

DEDICATION

To my peaceable kingdom:
Jim, David, Joan, Andy, Tracy,
and Elijah

ACKNOWLEDGMENTS

It is my good fortune to have friends who are skilled in many different areas; without them this book would never have been written.

Muriel Duncan is my trusted friend and colleague. I can't imagine trying to think my way through any topic of importance without talking to her. In this one, as always, she has been wise and generous.

Rose Tekel kept me going with helpful reminders about the writer's personality type. The fact she likes my Hanukkah tea rings gives me confidence.

Christel Markiewicz watches my stars. She predicted something creative this year. It's a source of hope no writer should be without.

Many marvellous dinners with Wanda and John Wallace, Kathy and Alan Aylett, Trisha Mills, Diana Goodwin, Sarah and David Tector, Carolyn and Mac Sinclair, Larry and Rhea Knapp, and the wonderful grown-up children of each of the above, have convinced me that meals shared with those we love are holy.

Karen Podolsky sent research on challah, and support. I am deeply blessed by my grandson's Fresno grandmother.

Jane Howe and Elizabeth Frazer provide bread for my soul, as do Ralph Johnston and the choir at St. Andrew's.

My mother believes no meal is complete without a slice of her daughter's homemade bread. In the same vein of high compliments, my children give tea rings to their friends. No writer could have better praise.

The staff at the North Bay Public Library offers cheerful and expert assistance, whether I am researching bread or murder mysteries. Suzanne and Bernie Brooks, along with their staff at Gulliver's Quality Books and Toys, know how to support their local authors, and I am grateful.

As always, it is a pleasure to work with the staff at Northstone. Editor Mike Schwartzentruber is both skilled and unfailingly patient with my second, third, and even fourth thoughts about a piece he thought was already finished. Margaret Kyle is an inspired designer, who has made this a series in which I am proud to be included. Verena Velten brought her special love of bread baking and design skills to this particular book. I am very grateful to all of them.

Thank you to Jim for knowing that firewood says "I love you" more clearly than roses, and for making sure that we never run out. There's no better way to keep a bowl of bread dough warm.

When I am in the kitchen, my grandmothers are always with me.

INTRODUCTION

I have an ancient cookbook that makes my children laugh. It came as a wedding present a long time ago. It contains my favourite bread recipes, with adaptations scribbled in pencil in the margins. The covers vanished long ago, and the most-used pages would make an archivist weep. They are torn and stained and so out of order I have to keep them in a plastic bag and lift them out carefully so they don't rip further.

But I love this book. When I pull it out of the cupboard, it makes me happy; it signals a slow morning in the kitchen and a floury expedition into sticky-fingered childhood.

I love to make bread.

I confess that I don't make it every season. In summer, for instance, when I want to keep the house cool, I simply buy good brown bread at the farmers' market. Even in winter, when it's good to warm the kitchen with an oven full of loaves, I am sometimes travelling or (terribly grown-up) preoccupied with work, and there's no room in my life for baking.

But when I can, week after week, I joyously make bread.

Which is why it can be called "spiritual." My dictionary says the word means "of, from, or relating to God; of, concerned with, or affecting the soul." Making bread affects my soul. It speaks to me of love and memory and holiness.

When my husband took a job that meant he would have to live in another city for several years, my first reaction was to fill the oven with multi-grain loaves jammed full of crunchy things – quinoa, oatmeal, oat bran, cornmeal, whole wheat flour – in order to stock the little fridge in his apartment.

This bread requires a sponge method to help it rise. (Mix warm water, yeast, molasses, and about a cup of flour, and let it sit in a warm place for a while. It gets quite spongy.) When I add the grains and knead for a long time, it seems to have sufficient energy to become, after baking, eight dense crunchy loaves that cover my kitchen counter and make me feel like Mother Earth.

When our grown-up children come home, a similar frenzy of mixing and kneading precedes their arrival. I make loaves of many kinds, stirring vats of soup on the stovetop while the bread bakes in the oven. Bread, it appears, speaks its own language: "I love you. Welcome home. Be well. Be strong. Remember me." After the children leave, I eat soup and bread for weeks, cherishing the echoes of their presence.

Bread goes with wine, which also speaks. My father made wine: parsnip wine, blueberry wine, rhubarb wine, chokecherry wine, even – in one spectacularly ill-considered experiment – pea pod wine. We teased him about drinking his garden, but it meant we had wine, white or red (or in the case of the pea pods, slightly green), to mark every celebration and to turn every dinner into a feast.

Dad felt his wine improved with age and when we left after a visit he always gave us a large bottle and an admonition to leave it alone for a year. We opened it within the week, of course. It tasted like my father's garden. Like home. No wonder so much religious ritual involves wine and bread. It speaks to us of gods who say, "Remember your true home."

In fact, bread is all about memories of home. For some, home might mean *naan*, slapped against the wall of a small outdoor oven to be pulled off gently when it is done. For others, home might mean a trip to the market to buy – always – not one but two baguettes, because one will be consumed on the way home. Some might remember a home where Navaho blue bread, from blue cornmeal, is baked to honour a baby's first laugh, and given to friends to encourage the child to grow up generous.

Bread is identity. It helps us remember who we are. My middle son – a veteran of many church suppers – says he arrived at the home of friends once, for a potluck supper, saw the casseroles and buns spread out on the table, and thought, "Ah! The food of my people." He and his siblings grew up calling cinnamon rolls Chelsea buns, which is what I learned to call them from my English grandmother. I learned to bake scones from her the English way, rich with currants, which some in my family dislike and leave in small rows on their plates like buckshot at a wild game supper.

Baking bread makes me calm, whether it is my English grandmother's scones or my Scottish grandmother's raised white loaves. Because bread is the opposite of fast food. You cannot make bread in ten minutes, and the slow work of kneading and shaping quiets our noisy and over-scheduled lives. Indeed, bread *demands* peace; you cannot grow grain in a battlefield. Bread also demands justice; cheap bread that results from the loss of the family farm is too bitter to eat.

In fact, bread is the very picture of the just society. In Dufferin Grove Park, in downtown Toronto, for instance, nearby residents use communal wood-fired outdoor bake ovens (built with city help) and by doing so create a neighbourhood where people gather to bake the breads their mothers taught them.

The great literary critic Northrop Frye, who lived not far from this neighbourhood, said the role of human imagination is to envision the "real form of human society hidden behind the one we see." Words, he said, shaped this vision, "revealed by philosophy and history and science and religion and law." That's true. It's why I wrote this book.

But the friends of the park who come to slide their loaves into those ovens *are* that vision. It is the same one offered by all great religions, where compassion and community prevail.

We have learned to see in bread an instrument of community between men – the flavour of bread shared has no equal.

~ Antoine de Saint-Exupery

My own faith expresses this vision by sharing bread and wine. Jesus called himself "the bread of life," and we remember him that way, as necessary as food. He called that "real form of human society" the kingdom of God.

Nothing is easy, of course. In a postmodern age when we question all our assumptions and struggle with global warming and belligerent politicians, the commonwealth of peace seems far away. But making bread gives us meaning. That, above all, is why it is a spiritual task. It helps us trust that the world will survive, that we are loved, that the kitchen where we work is holy ground.

There is no rational explanation for this. The healing power of kneading a lump of dough has nothing to do with the mind, and everything to do with the wisdom of the hands.

To eat bread without hope is still slowly to starve to death.

~ PEARL S. BUCK

15

Here, then, are stories and ideas about breads. You can consider them as you visit the local bakery. You can read this book for insights into women's lives, and into the realm of divinity and mystery, and for trust and hope in the wilderness of postmodern life.

Or you can just make a few simple loaves with it.

When I began to write this, I wondered what was left to say about bread's spiritual power. So many writers have luxuriated in print over the golden crust and sensual fragrance of a fresh-baked loaf. But at the height of my wondering, I had a dream. I was visited by a whole team of women, of which I seemed to be a member. I don't know what kind of team it was, but they all had Ph.D.'s, every one of them, and they were cheering me on. I take that to mean that there is still something to be said about bread. I hope this book is it.

[Breadbaking is] one of those almost hypnotic businesses, like a dance from some ancient ceremony. It leaves you filled with one of the world's sweetest smells... there is no chiropractic treatment, no Yoga exercise, no hour of meditation in a music-throbbing chapel, that will leave you emptier of bad thoughts than this homely ceremony of making bread.

~ M. F. K. Fisher, *The Art of Eating*

1
Bread as Language

Any celebration – Thanksgiving, Easter, pre-wedding gatherings, birthdays, or just the sheer joy of living – takes me to the kitchen, where I gather up flour and yeast, water and eggs, grains and seeds. I scoop and mix and knead, sticky-fingered and happy, until the dough is a smooth ball, which I place in a large bowl, cover with a clean tea towel, and deposit someplace warm.

And always there is this miracle: I discover I have grown calm. Making bread opens the door to a gentle place. I marvel that I do not go there every day.

These special meals are often held at the home of one or another of our dear friends. Traditions have attached themselves to every feast: Kathy's bunny cake at Easter, decorated with candy and licorice sticks by "children" now in their 20s and 30s; Wanda's pies at Thanksgiving, featuring North America's best pastry and the flesh of small, tender pumpkins.

It is my privilege to bring the bread — dinner rolls, or loaves of whole wheat or unbleached white flour, with eggs to make their texture very light, and toasted sesame seeds or poppy seeds sprinkled on top.

We gather around the table, often two tables put together. We say grace, holding hands. The host names and blesses any grown children who could not make it home. The empty chairs of absentees are filled by friends, new in-laws, and wide-eyed grandchildren. We rejoice in life's goodness and are grateful. And then we pour the wine and eat and laugh and talk for hours.

When the meal is over, our friends gather up leftovers and make sure elderly parents and returning students have generous packages to take with them. This feast, you see, is about more than pie or cake or wine or bread, although all those things are marvellous in their own right. It is about love.

No food says "I love you" more than bread. Love brings my friend Trisha to the door bearing soup and banana loaf, when she knows I am anxious. Love led my future daughter-in-law to ask how to make the cinnamon-laced breads of Christmas, although she is Jewish.

And love is the reason for this feast long ago.

No food says "I love you" more than bread.

21

It is just before the Pesach (Passover) holiday, the joyous week in which Jews celebrate their liberation from the land of Egypt. Jesus is in Bethany, near Jerusalem, and people have been dropping by to visit, including an eccentric with expensive ointment to smear on Jesus' head – too lovingly, some say.

Jesus is much admired. He has it in his head to celebrate the festival in the city. Two women volunteer to go early to get ready. They know what to do. The room Jesus has arranged for them must be swept clean of every crumb of leavened bread, because the food of the people who fled Egypt was the flat bread of the poor and the rushed and the overworked.

The women clean the large airy room once more, to be sure, and then prepare a feast: wine, chopped fruit, fish, and vegetables. And they make the wide, flat bread that is part of a proper Pesach meal – one part water, three parts flour, kneaded and gathered quickly in the hand, rolled thin and poked full of holes, then baked with a hot fire.

It takes all of one peaceful afternoon. Before they know it, Jesus and the others come smiling up the worn, mud brick steps. There is embracing and delight, because this is the year's holiest feast, the best collective memory of a nation with a thousand stories.

They gather round the table and bless the food and the ones who are not there, the ones they miss. They gratefully pour wine, eat, drink, and tell stories and laugh and drink more wine for a long time, because it is good to be together.

At the end, Jesus calls them to attention. They straighten up – they love him, and he is their teacher – because there is a note of ceremony in his voice, and something else. Sadness. Warning. They live, after all, in an occupied country and Jesus has been angry and visible.

He picks up a flat, fresh-baked loaf, and suddenly rips it to pieces. "This is my body," he says, "broken for you." He fills a cup with wine. "My blood, poured out for many."

His friends are stunned by this graphic portrayal of violence. But then Jesus smiles, as warmly as if this gesture had not happened. All will be well, he says, because the kingdom of God is near, where all have good fresh bread like this, and wine and honey in abundance.

They can see it then, as if the walls had dissolved around them. The peaceable kingdom, which cannot come unless it is first imagined. The commonwealth they must hold in their hearts until they can make it whole, until grandchildren on new unsteady legs come to a laden table, and thanks are said that all, all the world has bread.

24

Bread Says More than We Know

That 2000-year-old story set the Christian church on its often flawed and tumultuous way. And bread is at the centre of it, symbol of a prophet's torn body, and of the kingdom of God, where (more symbols) the lion will lie down with the lamb.

In a nation where many, including Jesus, were often hungry, what could be more compelling than to wrap the new religion in bread? What could draw more surely on the strength of Demeter, the reigning goddess of bread? Nothing could give Jesus' friends more hope – with his terrifying death soon to come – than bread, which depends on grain that dies in the fields but comes back again as goodness. At every mealtime, they would think of him. Every time they gathered as friends, he would be present in the breaking of bread.

That is more or less what happened. The story of that Passover (Pesach) meal has persisted for two millennia, with layers of meaning constantly being added.

I believe I saw another layer of that story in San Salvador, for instance: people lighting candles in a corner of the Metropolitan Cathedral that is dominated by a painting of a solemn, dark-robed man. This is the tomb of Archbishop Oscar Romero, the beloved priest who turned his back on the rich, after years of serving as their chaplain, to defend the poor during the assassinations and torture of the late 1970s.

There are people in the world so hungry that God cannot appear to them except in the form of bread.

- Mohandas Gandhi

Romero was gunned down in March 1980, riddled with bullets as he began a celebration of the mass – the ritualized wine and bread of Jesus' last meal with his friends.

The archbishop had preached against government-sponsored killings, the forced removal of peasants from the lands where they grew their corn. He had written to then-president Jimmy Carter pleading for an end to American military aid to El Salvador. Romero had been driven by the image of the peaceable kingdom, the same one imagined at a Passover meal 2000 years before.

I saw a similar vision in Sheshashit, Labrador, in 1985, when Innu families shared golden fry bread and caribou meat with reporters and sympathetic church visitors. We met in a large tent, sat on a carpet of fragrant spruce boughs and talked while the meal was cooked on a small wood stove. The elders were served, and then everyone else. Afterwards, we heard stories of low-flying NATO jets rehearsing war over Innu territory, frightening the children and the caribou.

The Innu, too, had a dream of peace. Three allied countries were paying Canada to let them use this land to practise the sort of low-level flights citizens of London and Frankfurt would not allow over their own soil. The flights continued for some years, but I have never forgotten the quiet speeches of the Innu, and their resolve, and the taste of bread in the Labrador bush.

So bread is resonant with meaning. When we place our hands in a bowl of sticky dough, we share a task with all those who make fry bread, or tortillas, or the flat bread of Pesach in a cloud of fear. Be strong, this bread says. Know who you are. The country of peace, which belongs to no one faith and to all of them, is not visible, but near.

The Multiple Meanings of Bread

The language of bread is audible, of course, in less dramatic settings. The confetti thrown at weddings (and detested by church janitors) was once rice. Before that, says Adrian Bailey in *The Blessings of Bread*, it began as the barley sprinkled around the temple of Demeter, a symbol of fertility no doubt appreciated by the bride and groom.

Similarly, the plea for money in the 1960s – "I need bread, man" – was a remnant of the ancient Egyptian custom of paying workers in bread, money having been not yet invented. The Egyptians measured the health of their economy by the fullness of their granaries. A little later, the Romans distributed their version of welfare cheques for the unemployed as loaves called *plebs frumentaria*, or corn commoners.

"He knows what side his bread is buttered on," we say knowingly of those who adjust their actions according to the current power structure. "Hunger never saw bad bread," and "Half a loaf is better than none," are proverbs that, for centuries, have hidden disappointment.

Before the invention of baking tins in England, the uncooked dough was simply placed on the floor of a hot oven, producing a black and dirty bottom crust for the servant, and, for the masters, a golden "upper crust" – a term we still use to distinguish those with diamonds from those without.

Even grinding grain into flour encapsulated wisdom. From the days when it was ground by water-turned mills comes a maxim for those who tempt fate: "The mill of the gods grinds slowly, but it grinds exceedingly fine."

Nothing better conveys the poignant power of the word "bread," though, than the phrase "bread and roses," immortalized in words sung by Judy Collins and others. The phrase originated on a sign that read, "We Want Bread And Roses Too!" It was carried by striking textile workers in January 1912, in Lawrence, Massachusetts, where dozens of factories produced more woollen and cotton goods than anywhere else in North America. The workers, mostly women, had been earning less than eight dollars a week when they received notice of a 32-cent pay cut – enough to cost them three loaves of bread out of an already stringent diet consisting mostly of bread, molasses, and beans.

At one point – worried by police brutality – the strikers began sending their children away, to be cared for by sympathizers in other parts of the country. After one contingent of about 90 children and their supporters marched with banners down New York City's Fifth Avenue, officials in Lawrence were furious. When 150 more children tried to leave by train for Philadelphia, police and militia waded in with clubs, beating and throwing women and their terrified offspring into paddy wagons.

But by then the tide had turned. In March, the companies settled, with the workers getting a raise in pay, and even overtime. Immigrants from 25 different countries had crossed cultural barriers in what was referred to ever after as the "Bread and Roses" strike.

The word "bread" had come to mean dignity.

When you have only two pennies left in the world, buy a loaf of bread with one, and a lily with the other.

~ Chinese Proverb

An Easy Bread for Celebrating Friendship

These raised, but not kneaded, rolls are very quick to make and seem to be received with as much gratitude as if they had taken all day. If you are not used to making bread, they are a good way to start. The flour can be unbleached white, or whole wheat. You can double the recipe if you have enough muffin tins, and bind yourself to your neighbours by giving them a dozen.

1 package instant dry yeast
2 tbsp. (30 mL) sugar
2¼ cups (560 mL) flour
1 tsp. (5 mL) salt
1 cup (250 mL) very warm water
1 egg
2 tbsp. (30 mL) soft shortening

Mix yeast with flour and sugar and salt in a large bowl. Stir in shortening and water, and then the egg. Mix. Cover with a tea towel and let rise in a warm place for about 30 minutes. Beat down and let rise again. Spoon dough into 12 greased muffin cups and sprinkle with sesame seeds or poppy seeds. Let rise again (about 20 minutes) and bake 15 to 20 minutes in a preheated 400°F (205°C) oven.

2
Bread as Identity

I learned to make bread in Schefferville, a mining town in northern Quebec. I was 25, the average age for this little community, which was accessible only by air or railway. There were no grandmothers, just young men and women and small children. Our bread arrived in a boxcar along with other perishables, all thoroughly stale by the time they were moved from truck to train and then made the (at best) 14-hour journey to the end of the line.

When I muttered one day about the unavailability of any bread that wasn't hard, white, pre-sliced, and smelling faintly of diesel fuel, a young woman from Newfoundland named Brenda Leyanaar invited me to her house. The art of making bread apparently still flourished where she came from, and she offered to teach me how.

We spent the afternoon mixing, inhaling wonderful smells, shaping, and baking. I arrived home with two fresh loaves and a lighter heart than I had known for some time. It wasn't just the bread I had been missing.

That was the beginning of a whole family history. Unlike many other young women in the community, I had no children. In fact, given the isolation of the town and my status as a woman without young dependents, I was soon conscripted to teach at the little English-speaking school. Supply teachers were few and far between. So I didn't bake many loaves that year, just a few experiments on weekends. I *did* break open my cookbooks at the bread section, though, and decided that no great mountain of learning is required to turn out a decent loaf.

A few years later, I had two children of my own, and – to my astonishment – two ovens in the rather well-equipped house in southern Quebec to which we had moved. I couldn't resist the challenge of producing something – anything – that would make use of these baker's riches. So I turned out loaves eight at a time, four from each oven, and discovered that kitchen counters covered with tidy, curve-topped golden bread made me very happy – a true mother, in fact, feeding her children from a large garden and a hot stove. For a young woman in the early 1970s, who was still firming up her identity (Who am I? someone's wife? someone's mother? a spouse-helpmate?), "bread-maker" became a title I could claim for my own.

I learned to make fancy breads to give away at Christmas, and dinner rolls to take as a hostess gift when invited out. My flourishing sense of self under this regime is illustrated by the way I produced four fragrant, braided circles of cinnamon-laced bread, gorgeously decorated, to thank the nurses at the hospital where I had given birth ten days before. Yes, indeed. Earth Mother *extraordinaire*. I have not yet figured out if this is something that should make me embarrassed (certainly I was a complete sucker for my husband's pride in my skill) or pleased.

Bread had become part of our family history. Sixteen years later, when the child whose birth had occasioned this yeast-driven frenzy spent a year in Australia, his pre-Christmas phone call was not a cry of loneliness, but a plea for the Christmas tea ring recipe. What would proclaim the holiday more than the familiar scent of cinnamon and yeast? Eight years later, his younger sister enlisted in Katimavik and spent a year crisscrossing Canada doing good and polishing her French. And, of course, baking bread, for which she phoned home to get directions. Later still, the oldest returned from Paris and took over the kitchen long enough to produce several baguettes.

When others remarked on this collective family talent (perhaps having observed that applause provoked more bread), we were assured in the face of what, to many, seemed to be a mystery. Our family was part of an informal guild restricted to those whose work allowed the flexibility bread-making demands, and whose personal history affirmed what others might think a waste of time. Instead of baking bread, in fact, I could have been taking courses to further my career, learning a language, or pursuing an advanced degree.

I did none of these things. I made bread. And in the quiet and contemplation it demanded, in the informal meditation it allowed – in the symbolism it carried – it was my salvation.

Talk of joy: there may be things better than beef stew and baked potatoes and home-made bread – there may be.

~ DAVID GRAYSON

39

A Fast History of Bread

To tell the story of bread, you have to begin with wild wheat grasses, gathered and crushed with a handheld pestle and mortar in Mesopotamia soon after the great ice sheets receded. The first cultivated wheat was einkorn, very high in protein but not easily adaptable to the rich plains of Egypt, where large-scale farming – thanks to the fluctuating Nile – was getting underway as early as 5000 BCE. Emmer wheat thrived on the fertile plain (and is still grown today in Italy by some farmers who admire its high protein and usefulness for pasta). By about 3000 BCE, the Egyptians had invented a closed oven and were using bread and beer as money.

Meantime, in India, grain was cultivated along the Indus River valley, at least by 2300 BCE. In Britain, barley and oats made what is now the south of England an agricultural centre by 1050 BCE, and by 500 BCE wheat had made its way westward as well.

By 1000 BCE, Rome had fallen in love with yeasted bread. They fermented the dough with wheat bran – soaked in wine and sun-dried – and improved the dough's whiteness by adding chalk. Later, public bakeries produced thousands of loaves daily. Enterprising politicians distributed bread at low cost, and finally, in 41 BCE, for free.

Egyptian Wall Painting of a Harvesting Scene from the Tomb of Sennedjem

Although it's easy to focus on the Middle East as the major source of cereal grains – especially for bread – our ancestors were busily developing grains in other places at the same time. Rice was grown in the Far East from about 6000 BCE. Tiny, prehistoric cobs of corn dating back to 5000 BCE were found in the early 1960s in Tehuacán, Mexico.

But bread as we think of it in North America – that is, raised bread – began, many believe, in Egypt around 3000 BCE. Beer may have been used as leaven. Or perhaps wild yeast permeated a mixture of meal and water. Certainly that process continues to be useful. Sourdough – made by leaving dough open to spores that are naturally present in the air – remains a viable and profitable way of making bread.

Acorns were good until bread was found.

~ Francis Bacon

Modern Sourdough

Boudin's bakery in San Francisco, for example, makes excellent use of a French baking technique and local wild organisms captured from the air, in a starter mix that began 150 years ago. San Francisco is my favourite American city, perhaps because Eli lives there – Elijah to be exact, my grandson, of huge dark eyes and (at our last visit) solemn three-week-old face – and, oh yes, our daughter-in-law and eldest son, his parents.

I love the ocean climate and the hilly streets with inclines to which Montreal – despite Mount Royal – can only aspire. And I love the bread. San Francisco's cool, often foggy weather and the unique combination of wild yeast and bacteria (*candida humilis* and *lactobacillus sanfrancisco*) cooperate to produce in every loaf of this sourdough bread a taste like no other.

When Eli's parents were married, they left a simple loaf of San Francisco sourdough in each of their guest's hotel rooms, ready for tearing off and chewing by the flavourful hunk. So five years later, when we went to meet Eli for the first time, we naturally went to Boudin's.

We walked around and inhaled and had sandwiches for lunch. Eli peered briefly out of a pouch on his daddy's chest, and then fell back to sleep, never seeing the big baskets of bread slowly drifting by on a conveyor belt, or the big racks sliding into the gas-fired ovens, or the "bread museum." It was there, in the bread museum, that the new parents, with delighted grins, pointed out the story of the *Kretenwegge*, a six-foot-long loaf traditionally made in the Twente district of Holland by the neighbours of a new mother, so she wouldn't have to bake for a week.

Bread, it seems, is part of every story. Weddings. Births. Picnics. Parties. In our church back home – as in every church, I think – women make sandwiches for every funeral. People eat them standing up, waiting in line to hug the grieving ones, or they pull up a chair and visit with each other, one last celebration for their friend.

After we say goodbye to San Francisco at the airport, hugging the tiny child and his parents, we discover racks of sourdough bread for sale, all up and down the concourse, extra bits of memory to take home.

In Paris today millions of pounds of bread are sold daily, made during the previous night by those strange, half-naked beings one glimpses through cellar windows, whose wild-seeming cries floating out of those depths always makes a painful impression. In the morning, one sees these pale men, still white with flour, carrying a loaf under one arm, going off to rest and gather new strength to renew their hard and useful labour when night comes again. I have always highly esteemed the brave and humble workers who labour all night to produce those soft but crusty loaves that look more like cake than bread.

~ ALEXANDRE DUMAS, FRENCH WRITER (1802-1870)

A Dream of Bread

It's a familiar story to many. Pharaoh, the divine ruler of Egypt, has an indecipherable dream. You can imagine how it was: the sacred leader of the most advanced society in the ancient world, his subjects' well-being inextricably tied to his own, is troubled by a dream that no one can interpret.

They lived on dreams back then. The waking and sleeping worlds informed each other, two different realities that were equally important. Even today, we would know that when a man dreams that he is standing on the banks of the holy river Nile, watching seven fat cows rise up out of the water followed by seven "ugly and gaunt" cows who devour them – even today, we would know that something significant has just risen out of this man's unconscious. Water is a useful symbol for the depths of every human soul.

But this man is the pharaoh. And nobody can tell him what his dream means. Or perhaps they are afraid to say, him being a god and all, with the power of their life and death in his hands.

Then Pharaoh dreams again, this time more prosaically, of a single stalk of wheat with seven heads of grain sprouting from it. Again, the dream shifts uncontrollably into a bleaker image. Seven heads of grain, "thin and scorched by the east wind," swallow up the healthy ones.

Wind in a dream – even in the 21st century – still alerts the practised dreamer. Breath of the Spirit. The winds of God. It seems that a deity of higher divinity than even the ruler of Egypt is talking.

His magicians still apparently mystified, Pharaoh's chief cupbearer steps forward. (How many cupbearers did he have? I wonder if they gathered up his cups, as my small children did for me when I would wander the house thinking, leaving my coffee on bookshelves to grow cold and sometimes mouldy.) He begins apologetically with his own "shortcomings," which had earlier placed him, along with Pharaoh's chief baker, in the dungeon of the captain of the guard.

"Another prisoner, his name is Joseph, explained our dreams to us," the cupbearer says, "and things turned out exactly as he said. I was restored to my position, and the baker" – the cup-bearer pauses for a moment – "the baker was hanged."

"Bring the prisoner," says Pharaoh.

There is much rushing about to make Joseph presentable. A shave is ordered. Fresh clothes are provided. The Hebrew slave is brought before the ruler of all Egypt.

JOSEPH INTERPRETING
PHARAOH'S DREAM, 1897
BY REGINALD ARTHUR

Joseph hears the dream, takes a breath, and tells the truth, which, given the fate of the chief baker, seems a serious risk.

But Pharaoh listens calmly to Joseph's interpretation.

"A major famine is coming," Joseph says. "It will last seven years. But before that will be seven years of harvests as fat and as rich as your seven dream-cows that rose dripping from your sacred river."

Then Joseph – ludicrously brave – gives the god of Egypt what sounds like an order. "You must build granaries to store this grain. There will be enough to last for all the famine years," he says, "and you must feed your people."

What follows is as astonishing as if George W. Bush suddenly made Michael Moore vice-president, telling him to run the country as he sees fit. Pharaoh ignores his usual advisors, places his own ring on the finger of this young foreigner – not even an Egyptian – and puts him in charge of everything.

That's how important bread was. Workers were paid in bread. Egyptian soldiers ate four pounds of it a day. Bread was placed in tombs for use in the afterlife. Now it was the salvation of an oppressed people, because the Hebrews rose in status with Joseph, and prospered in the land of Egypt.

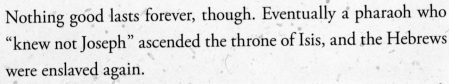

Nothing good lasts forever, though. Eventually a pharaoh who "knew not Joseph" ascended the throne of Isis, and the Hebrews were enslaved again.

They finally had to rush after Moses into the desert, taking with them the bread that became emblematic of their journey; bread that had not risen, the antithesis of the beloved bread of the Egyptians. Bread that would mark the Passover feast of the liberation. Bread that showed they were becoming, once again, themselves.

Because for the ancient Israelites, and for us today, bread is identity. How we change our lives in order to make room for its preparation, how we feed our families and guests, what kind of bread we choose to buy or how we bake it: bread tells us who we are.

The challah bread, for instance, the sweet egg bread of the Jewish Shabbat, is a powerful symbol of identity. It is preceded into the hot oven by a tiny chunk of the dough, a symbol of the first piece set aside for the priests in the ancient days of the temple.

Sesame seeds are sprinkled on top, as a reminder of the manna by which the Hebrews were fed in the desert. And challah is salted just a little before eating, to remind the people of the admonition in Genesis that "by the sweat of your brow shall you get bread to eat."

Bread is identity for me as well. I chose a slow life, unobtrusive. Making bread symbolized that choice. I stayed at home writing my articles, leaving my coffee cups around the house, cooking soup, making loaves that required the whole day. I had abundant time between risings, though, to sit at a computer, interview people, edit stories, and consider the meaning of dreams.

This is not a choice everyone can make. It wasn't even a conscious one for me. It's only looking back now that I can see I chose a less-lucrative existence, a less-ambitious course, a life that owed as much to my stoic Scottish grandmother as to the feminist peers with whom I was of one mind.

There's no help for it now. I don't know that I was right. Certainly I could only do this with a trustworthy and gainfully employed spouse. Choosing to live in such deep economic dependence on another is counter-intuitive in today's world. But it let me garden, and bake bread.

The danger is not lest the soul should doubt whether there is any bread, but lest, by a lie, it should persuade itself that it is not hungry.

~ SIMONE WEIL

53

The Consequence of Bread

The history of civilization itself depends on bread. The availability of grain that was 15 percent protein (the emmer wheat of the pharaohs), that could be stored for years — especially with the help of cats to keep the rodents in check — affected both war and peace. It could be poured as grain into the hold of a ship. Baked, it could be carried in a soldier's knapsack. It was once rumoured that baguettes were invented to be carried in the trousers of Napoleon's solders on the Russian campaign, but apparently — since the bread's unique texture depended on a technique developed only later in Vienna — this story is not true.

Even without war, legislation around bread affected vast populations. London saw riots when the Corn Laws were passed in 1815, protecting the price of grain for English farmers by raising the duty on imported wheat, and making bread unattainable for the poor. The laws were not repealed until 1846; the people suffered greatly.

In fact, bread itself (and other agricultural products) may be partly to blame for the social inequalities and class identities that lead to war. According to Ronald Wright, in *A Short History of Progress*, early farming communities were as egalitarian as the hunter-gatherer societies, in which "it was easy to vote with one's feet" if a leader tried to get too uppity. But the ability to grow grain and to feed the people bread meant well-nourished, flour-

ishing populations. More people meant less land to go around.
Land – required to grow the grain – became more precious.
Some figured out ways to accumulate it. "Differences in wealth
and power became entrenched," Wright explains. "Early farmers
along the Danube left only tools in their remains; later settlements are heavily fortified and strewn with weapons."

But whenever peace prevailed, the ability to grow and store
grain and make bread meant leisure. Towns could be built,
because food – corn, rice, wheat, barley, rye – grown outside the
walls could feed many more people than were needed to produce

Everyone is kneaded out of the same dough but not baked in the same oven.

- Yiddish Proverb

it. Surpluses meant stability in times of need, as Joseph and Pharaoh had learned. Leisure for learning meant coliseums, markets, trade, merchants, architecture, universities, libraries, sculpture, salons, patrons of the arts, churches, cathedrals, and eventually, physics, engineering, aeronautics.

One day, it would build the plane that carries me to see Elijah and his parents.

A Simple White Loaf

In 1307, British bakers separated into those who baked white bread and those who baked brown, with peasants generally getting the brown. Even earlier, in Rome, the aristocracy had loved their pure white bread, leaving the coarser loaves for the poor.

The fibre in a whole wheat loaf is very good, of course. But if you are not used to baking bread, this white loaf rises dependably. It is delicious, especially toasted. With freezer raspberry jam, or suitably embellished with cheese or peanut butter, it provides pure giddy decadence.

This loaf doesn't keep well, but freezes beautifully; and, like most bread recipes, it can be doubled.

2 tbsp. (30 mL) active dry yeast
  (or 2 envelopes)
2¼ cups (560 mL) lukewarm water
2 tbsp. (30 mL) sugar
1 tbsp. (15 mL) salt
6–7 cups (1.5–1.75 L) unbleached all-
  purpose flour or bread flour

Combine yeast, water, and sugar in a large bowl. Mix well and add salt. Let stand for a few minutes while you measure out the flour and grease a baking sheet, sprinkling it with cornmeal or lining it with parchment paper.

Add 4 cups (1 L) of flour, mix, and then beat for about 100 strokes, adding more flour until the dough is firm enough to turn out onto a lightly floured counter (well scrubbed ahead of time) or bread board. Knead until dough is smooth and elastic – about 10 minutes – adding more flour as needed. You may not require the entire 7 cups (1.75 L); much depends on the moisture in the air and flour.

Let sit while you wash out the large bowl and oil it. Put the ball of dough in the bowl, turn it so the oil coats all sides, and cover with a clean tea towel. Let rise in a warm place, about an hour and a half. I often fill my double sinks with very hot water, put the oven rack over them, and put the bowl on top. Fine if no one wants to use the sink.

Once the dough has risen, punch it down. Very satisfying. If children are available, they will joyfully take on this task.

Shape the dough into two round loaves and place on the baking sheet. Carve an X across the top of each loaf with the sharpest knife you have, and spray with water or vinegar. Sprinkle with poppy seeds or sesame seeds. I like to do one of each, which impresses guests.

Put on the middle rack of a cold oven, heat to 400°F (205°C), and bake for about 45 minutes. Loaves should be rich brown and sound hollow when tapped. Cool on a rack, or find something to prop them up slightly, so the air circulates around them.

3

Bread as Trust and Courage

Bread that has been made over an open fire in the bush tastes wonderful, spiced with hunger and essence of smoke. When Jim and I go canoeing, mostly we make pancakes as our bread, because it's easy to carry a dry mix made ahead of time. For us, these flat golden breads are flavoured with memory as well. When we took our small children camping, years ago, they were delighted by mixing the batter, and by learning to turn pancakes in the hot skillet. They especially admired their father's skill at tossing half-baked pancakes in the air so they would flip on the way back down to the pan. The fact that he sometimes missed and had to rescue a flat cake covered in pine needles in no way diminished their awe and pleasure.

Jim and I still make pancakes on canoe trips, and remember those days with our young children and tell each other that, yes, we *were* good parents. We loved making pancakes with them at breakfast. Or, using an ingenious rack, we taught them to toast bread over an open fire. They learned to make biscuits in a

reflector oven, a skilled process requiring a hot fire. Or, equally difficult, they mastered making them in a pan raised on small stones, inside a large cast-iron pot placed in the fire and heaped with coals.

Often, hungry from the day's adventures, we all made twisters at bedtime – biscuit dough wrapped on the end of a long stick and held close to the coals until it is pale brown, then twisted off, leaving a convenient hole for jam or honey.

Now, years later, our breakfast before a day's paddle is food for the journey, real and physical and intensely metaphorical all at once. We are competent outdoors people, this golden delicious hot-bread-in-the-wilderness says. Never mind that we stop to rest more often every year.

Once, on such a trip, I dreamed of my paternal grandfather standing near the campfire, looking approvingly at a laden skillet, his shapeless felt hat tilted on his head. In real life, he had emigrated from England and had hacked out a farm in Northern Ontario – too far north, my own father once told me, to produce much except pulp and venison. Still, the family survived. I scarcely knew that grandfather, since he died when I was five.

But I knew who this dream-figure was, and I knew there was a message in his presence. We can do what our forefathers did, we can survive on very little, we can live in a land that is unknown to us, we can move on. Living, even briefly, as our ancestors did in the past, relying on ancient skills – such as making bread on an open fire – helps to make us confident today.

To be sensual, I think, is to respect and rejoice in the force of life, of life itself, and to be present in all that one does, from the effort of loving to the making of bread.

– James A. Baldwin

Such trust in our ability to accomplish what we are called to do is hard to come by. It requires courage, which is as much gift, I believe, as accomplishment. Courage comes by grace from God, if we go out to meet it. Courage is woven through the three stories that follow.

Elijah and Ravens

One of Israel's great prophets, Elijah, is ordered by God to tell rebellious King Ahab that there will be "neither dew nor rain these years, except by my word." Elijah obeys, confronting his king with the message designed to bring the monarch into line.

But apparently the non-anxious leadership style displayed by Pharaoh when confronted with a similar disaster is not shared by Israel's king.

Elijah leaves the king and returns home, almost too frightened to sleep. Finally, he drifts off, but is awakened – or is he still dreaming? – by a voice: "Elijah. Get up. Go! You must hide by the Wadi Cherith, which is east of the Jordan." Elijah gets up and begins to walk. Finally, he arrives and sets himself up in a humble tent by the almost-dry waterway, wondering how he is to survive in such a wilderness.

But morning after morning, evening after evening, he hears a great whistling of wings, and raucous calls; and then ravens float down, huge and black, their wrinkled talons clutching meat and bread for him to eat.

Elijah eats and paces, hides and sleeps and mutters to his God. He goes down into the wadi and drinks the tiny trickle of water it sustains, until that, too, disappears under the onslaught of eternal sunshine. And then God whispers again…

God has lured Elijah into courage, ordering him to scold a king who could order his death at any moment, and then placing him on a straight path into a desert. But then God sends those ravens. The bread they bring does more than ease his aching belly, important though that is. Elijah has to trust that they will arrive; he has to learn patience, and keep his courage up. He will need God's daily bread of courage to sustain him in a wilderness where each sunrise brings its own hungers.

I think that's why we pack our pancake mix and coffee and dried soup and go canoeing. It's a way to study what Elijah learned. Like him, we use our bodies for propulsion, getting around this water-ridden country the old way. We paddle until we run out of water, then hike along the portages, called *onigum* by the Anishinabe who have used them for 5000 years. These paths are well-trodden and logical, always the wisest route to take, and we feel the presence of the ancient ones beside us.

Like Elijah, we are learning courage. Wilderness lies just ahead in every life. We may be anguished by a loved one's illness or our own, or stressed at work, or disappointed in our dreams. We all will face old age, the last frontier. We need to trust that God will send the ravens, or their kin, with bread to give us strength.

For many years, an elderly friend appeared at our door every few weeks with one simple white loaf. He had learned to bake bread in his retirement. It often arrived at the perfect moment, as if he somehow knew that stressed parents and their boundary-testing teens needed just this time together in the kitchen, peacefully talking over warm home-made bread and strawberry jam. As if he knew we needed comfort.

After a long day of paddling, Jim and I find a place to sleep. In the morning, we build a fire and cook, slowly, with pleasure. We wash down fresh-cooked, syrup-laden cakes with coffee, and rejoice that we are fed in soul and body both at once.

BREAD AND STONES

Sheer hunger, as much as smoky flavour, makes bread delicious in the bush. When Jesus, gone to fast for 40 days, was told that he should turn stones into bread if he really was the son of God, it must have been a huge temptation. It's an enigmatic, fascinating story.

Jesus rises dripping from the muddy Jordan, and a dove drops to his shoulder, swift as a hawk, but gentle. A voice says, "This is my Son, the Beloved, with whom I am well pleased."

Then Jesus embraces his friend John the Baptizer and walks away into the desert. He sleeps wrapped in his cloak against the cold night air, and meditates for days, and is, naturally, starving. Then, one night, out of the darkness comes a different voice, that of the fallen angel known as Satan: "If you really are the son of God, command these stones to become loaves of bread."

Jesus tosses back a scholarly quote: "One does not live by bread alone, but by every word that comes from the mouth of God."

But more temptations fall softly out of the night: "Here we are on a mountain, throw yourself off, your God will send angels to save you." And later: "Here, I will give you all the kingdoms in the world, if you will worship me…"

"Away with you," says Jesus. There is empty silence. Suddenly, the angels *do* appear and, singing, bring him food. He goes to Galilee then, and makes friends with fishers, teaching and healing any who come looking for his skills.

CHRIST IN THE DESERT
BY IVAN NIKOLAEVIC KRAMSKÖJ

Jesus is not known for fasting. Later in his career he eats and drinks with tax collectors and other sinners and is called a glutton and a drunkard. He is so concerned for the pleasure of wedding guests that he turns water into wine; and he incurs the anger of his religious peers by picking corn on the Sabbath.

But first he leaves his friends and goes to starve in the wilderness. Perhaps his vigil and debate with Satan is a vision quest, a necessary effort to discern what shape his life should take. In hallucinations rising out of hunger, he may find wisdom.

Perhaps, like Elijah, he is learning courage. Jesus tells Satan firmly that bread alone is not enough, that God's commandments of compassion and love and justice are crucial for human life. Later, the people will want Jesus to launch a coup against the Romans, perhaps. They may want bread and circuses, or magic to show up rival gods. Standing against these temptations will be hard. Satan is merely a prompter for a larger drama; Jesus is rehearsing the brave heart that he will need.

In fact, this time in the wilderness may simply be an initiation. If Jesus can survive the rustles of the night, small creatures scurrying in the dark that sound like large ones, he will be brave enough to challenge authority. If he can wrestle with the call to power and easy glory, and survive with his soul intact, he will be a grown-up. More than that, he will be a prophet wise enough to lead his people into a new way of seeing the world, in which bread is only one half of what we need. The courage to point to the compassionate kingdom, and to declare its absolute priority, is the other half.

Grace is available for each of us every day - our spiritual daily bread - but we've got to remember to ask for it with a grateful heart and not worry about whether there will be enough for tomorrow.

– SARAH BAN BREATHNACH

Corn in the Wilderness

An Ojibway story about corn also relies on the bread of courage.

Wunzh embraces his friends and walks away into the wilderness. He will stay here for days. Stifling his hunger, he waits quietly in a small clearing for the spirit-guide he knows will appear. Finally, a figure dressed in green emerges from the trees along the skyline. "My name is Mondawmin," the figure says, and offers in a friendly way to wrestle.

Each night, Mondawmin appears late in the evening, and he and Wunzh struggle until dawn, both of them strong and determined. But after the third night, Mondawmin lies dying. He tells Wunzh his last wish: "Take off my clothes and place me in the earth. Tend my grave with care."

Wunzh, bereft, does so faithfully for weeks. And then, one day, a small green shoot pokes through the dark earth. Soon green plumes are rising toward the sky and finally a tall plant – as tall as Mondawmin, with shining hair like his – stands in the little clearing. And Wunzh knows his friend has returned, bringing the gift of corn.

Courage does not come by simply waiting. Wunzh receives the gift of corn by willingly wrestling with the stranger who becomes his friend, and willingly tending his grave. In fact, the

protagonists in all three stories wrestled with some eagerness: Elijah with his fear, Jesus with temptation, and Wunzh with his spirit-guide. In their willingness to find wisdom by living in a harsh place without food, they offer insight for our own fraught moments, when we are tempted to give up. They teach us to trust that bread in some form will arrive; that we will be given the heart to wrestle with life's necessary crises.

These stories might even help us be brothers and sisters with the ancient ones who were here before the Europeans came, the ones who grew the corn that was the gift of Mondawmin. Five hundred years ago, they taught the strangers how to grow it too.

It's one more reason, I suppose, for going into wilderness, for walking on trails made long before my British grandparents sailed to this new home. I want to learn the spirituality of the people who were here already.

They knew that Creation was the result of many creatures working together – a woman who fell from the sky, for instance, and a turtle who sheltered her, and an otter who dove over and over to carry up the first piece of land. They told of ravens and coyotes playing tricks on humans; and of Wunzh and his spirit-guide, wrestling for the sake of corn.

That's quite different, as

AZTEC WOMEN MAKING BREAD
BY GALLO GALLINA

Thomas King explains in *The Truth about Stories*: *A Native Narrative,* from my ancestors' god who organized Creation by himself. "All creative power is vested in a single deity who is omnipotent, omniscient, and omnipresent… creation is a solitary, individual act."

76

The disparity is vast. But I believe even newcomers – like me – can see some things we share. Sometimes, kneading my bread in my tidy little kitchen, sometimes I hear ravens outside, calling from one swooping power line to another. They make me think of old Elijah, watching them drift toward him through the evening sky, like huge dark kites carrying bread.

But they also make me think of ravens in Native stories, rattling their black wings outside my window, sly wise creatures playing jokes. Perhaps Elijah's ravens were like them – tricksters bringing bread to a trembling human, winking and stepping out of reach to see Elijah chase them. These ravens might move from the stories of one ancient people to the stories of another and end up in the present.

I listen to their raucous voices and wonder if the gods of the people who were here at first, and mine, could talk to one another. "In our Native story," says King, the world is at peace…" Perhaps that is the same landscape of peace Jesus dreamed of with his friends, the one where there is bread enough for all.

Perhaps the bread-god Jesus and the green-clad warrior Mondawmin, who died to bring the corn, are not so far apart.

A crust eaten in peace is better than a banquet partaken in anxiety.

~ Aesop

CORNBREAD

My children, I hope, would tell you this; I always gave them a good breakfast. One of our favourites was cornbread, baked in the cast-iron frying pan in a very hot oven, and served with jam or maple syrup and some fruit, and cheese to bump up the morning protein.

All cornbreads are quick, baked at a very high temperature, and easy to make. If there is any left over from breakfast, the first person through the door at the end of the day can split it, toast it, and spread it with peanut butter to keep them alive until suppertime.

Stoneground cornmeal is superior in flavour and nutrition – more of the germ is retained – but it doesn't keep as well as that ground by huge steel rollers. Search it out in health food stores (and some supermarkets) and store it in the fridge for no more than four months.

If you have a couple of 9-inch round or square cake tins, this recipe can be doubled for a large or hungry breakfast crowd. You'll have no trouble using it all.

1 ½ cups (375 mL) buttermilk
2 eggs
1 cup (250 mL) cornmeal
½ cup (125 mL) flour
    (whole wheat or unbleached)
2 tbsp. (30 mL) sugar
3 tsp. (15 mL) baking powder
3 tbsp. (45 mL) butter
a dash of salt

Heat oven to 450°F (230°C). Beat eggs and buttermilk together. In a separate bowl, mix dry ingredients. Put the butter in the frying pan and then in the oven until melted, then twirl the pan so it coats the sides. Pour what's left into the buttermilk mixture and stir. Fold that mixture into the dry ingredients, but don't overmix.

    Put the whole thing into the frying pan and bake for about 30 minutes on the middle rack. (I test it at 20 minutes, poking a toothpick into the centre.)

    Turn out on a board or large plate and serve.

4

Bread as Memory

My grandmother made bread in a large, white, smooth bowl. I don't remember her doing that, although I remember the small second-story apartment where she lived, and the cast-iron parlour stove that burned coal. My aunts and my mother would smoke and talk with my grandmother, gathered around the big dining table. I would listen while sweeping, or playing with, the ashes that fell beneath the stove – a five-year-old Cinderella with a whisk.

Although my own mother was rightly proud of her other skills in the kitchen, she did not make bread. Today, when I ask her why (at 93, she is beyond regrets about what she did or didn't do), she answers with memories: first, of my grandmother making bread every two or three days, four loaves at a time, always during the week. "She would put the yeast cake in warm water at night, and then in the morning would mix it in the crock, and then it was an all-day thing."

In fact, hot bread would come out of my grandmother's oven just as her four daughters arrived home from school, although that was not the reason for the timing. "Everything was done to suit your grandfather," my mother explains to me. "If your grandmother got mad at him, she wouldn't bake bread. She'd send us to the store, where we bought two loaves, stuck together, for 35 cents. It was always white bread. She never bought anything else, or made anything else."

My mother looks back, remembering the bread as clearly as if it was yesterday. She remembers, for example, the way hot bread in the oven made her eyes sting. The way the flour was delivered in enormous bags and stored in the oak cupboard in the kitchen. The way the oil had to be worked into every corner of the bread tins (which every baker used, and the manufacture of which sustained the Cornwall tin mines). That was my mother's job, oiling the tins.

And she remembers the day – married, then, with young children – she attempted to bake bread on her own. When my older brother declared it to be "like a brick," she decided she would never do it again. "If I couldn't make bread like my mother, I wouldn't make it. She always got first prize for her bread at the fair." My mother's voice is full of emotion as she says this. I don't know if it is envy or loss, love or pride.

I suppose – in the complicated mother-daughter dynamic with which my mother and I still struggle mightily – her decision to avoid bread-making freed me, later, to become the baker. When my grandmother died, I inherited her large white bowl and for many years made bread in it. Each time, I would see my grandmother before me, a strong, quiet, Scottish woman, who adored her grandchildren and never once complained about a life that was, at times, difficult.

But one chilly day, too rushed to be making bread, I slid the white bowl into a slightly warm oven to keep the dough safe from draughts. Then I heated the oven for the batch of bread, forgetting that the bowl was still there. It cracked with the high temperature.

My grandmother had died years before, but that was the day I lost her.

My daughter, a student, arrived home a few months later and proudly handed me a large parcel. She had searched Montreal, where she lived, and found a replacement for the bowl – not quite as large, not quite as old, but brimming over with significance.

You can't guarantee the carriers of memory. Nothing, especially not a fragile piece of English ironstone, lasts forever. But you can – oh yes – you *can* distribute love with small gestures, like a loaf of bread, or a smooth white bowl to make it in.

My mother, when she comes for dinner, always asks the same question: "Did you make this bread?" If I answer yes, her satisfaction is as tangible as the loaf that is sliced before her.

Bread's Ancient Wisdom

Generations of women are connected through bread. I remember my friend Birdie's raised doughnuts, when, years ago, I visited my husband-to-be at the Frazer ranch in southern Saskatchewan. When I left for Moose Jaw to catch the train back East, she handed me a brown paper bag containing a dozen exquisite sugar-dusted doughnuts, the ones she made for the men on horseback, moving cattle. Already suffering from loneliness, I ate them all before the train had left the station.

And there's my friend Diana's panettone. Every Easter morning, she appears quietly at the door. On her way home from the sunrise service, she has swung by to drop off her special bread made in a coffee can, rich with mixed fruit, and tall, with a golden and rounded mushroom-shaped top that spells holidays and good toast.

Before Diana, came our mutual friend Wanda, who arrived Maundy Thursday evening with a basket of small, perfect buns, spicy and fragrant and marked with a cross for Good Friday morning.

Both breads commemorate the death and resurrection of the bread-god, Jesus, 2000 years

ago. But these gifts are also in some way about a bread-goddess who preceded Jesus by seven centuries. It's the story of a mother and a daughter, and a love strong enough to cross the boundary between death and life.

The screams vibrate through a sunny field of crocus and narcissus. The beautiful Persephone, gathering flowers with her friends, is swept by Hades, ruler of the underworld, into his golden chariot and carried to his kingdom of the dead to be his Queen.

Persephone's mother, Demeter, the powerful goddess of grain, hears her pleas for help, but cannot find her. Filled with rage, keening for her child, Demeter plunges the world into endless winter. Disguised as a servant, she wanders to the city of Eleusis and is welcomed by Queen Metaneira. Unaware that she is entertaining a goddess, the Queen gives her baby son into Demeter's care. But when she discovers Demeter holding the little prince by his heel in the fire (in gratitude, she is immortalizing him) more screams ensue, until Demeter, profoundly insulted, reveals her goddess-self.

In compensation, the people build Demeter a temple. She locks herself into it and wallows in depression, fiercely disallowing the arrival of spring. Zeus, king of the gods, intervenes with pleading messengers. Demeter is unmoved. Finally, Zeus orders the young Persephone restored to her mother. But Hades loves her profoundly and, thanks to his wiles, Persephone must return to the underground for one-third of every year. Even so, each spring mother and daughter are reunited and the fields come to life.

The Return of Persephone, c. 1891 by Frederic Leighton

Any mother can understand how this goddess of both bread and the fertile earth could be the focus of a religion as powerful in its time as any religion today. The story is compelling. I love my daughter, who lives a continent away. I cherish our visits. And once in a while we revisit, laughing now, the occasion one September when I got a call from her worried colleague saying, "We don't know where Tracy is."

She'd been arrested by the Royal Canadian Mounted Police, while photographing their activities in Burnt Church, New Brunswick. Native fishers were taking lobster in accordance with a Supreme Court decision allowing them to do so, but government officials and local non-Native fishers were taking an opposite view. Tempers were running high. Tracy had gone out in a Native boat as a human rights observer and – camera held high – had kept it going while their craft was deliberately rammed and all on board were dumped into the chilly waters of Miramichi Bay. Police divers had leapt overboard, pulled them out, and handcuffed them.

The Native people had been taken to jail and locked up right away. But when the RCMP discovered their haul included a young, white, human rights activist, they began moving her from place to place, by boat and by police car. (I believe they were trying to figure out what to do with her.) And since no one *except* the RCMP knew where she was, her co-workers became anxious.

For me and my husband, it is mark of honour to be arrested on a principle of human rights. So I was proud and perfectly calm until a friend called to commiserate, and – never having met my daughter – asked gently how old she was. "Twenty-one," I said, and burst into tears.

Demeter had come to life. I raged helplessly around the house. Tracy was released in a matter of hours. Meantime, I would have conjured endless winter, if I could have.

Mother-daughter affection does not stop there. My friends Diana and Wanda and Kathy and Sarah love their daughters, and we love each other's daughters as if they were our own, rejoicing in weddings or babies or graduations, and seeking ways to help in a crisis. These relationships between generations of women are complex and mysterious, and strong. Just as Jesus, the beloved son, is not to be separated from his father, so this goddess of the earth and of bread will not be estranged from her daughter.

The Mighty Gods of Bread

Those who worshipped Demeter knew they belonged to a powerful and complicated goddess. All of Greece revered her. Each year, from about the seventh century BCE to the fourth century CE — over a thousand years — thousands of pilgrims made the journey from Athens to her temple in Eleusis, pausing for rituals along the way.

H. K. Jacob explains, in *Six Thousand Years of Bread*, how, once in the sacred city, blindfolded novitiates entered a terrifying passion play involving a fierce monster, steaming mud, and hours of darkness. But when the blindfolds were removed, the novitiates were welcomed with bright torchlight, clean white garments, and shouts of joy: "Welcome to the sanctuary, bridegroom." When "the novitiates raised their eyes," says Jacob, "they beheld a smiling little girl standing at the altar of Demeter. It was a child who performed the priestly services!"

It's a gentle picture of a commanding goddess; and Demeter's continuing strength as a religion meant that Christianity as a new religion struggled greatly with her. But conquering Goths finally sacked her temple at Eleusis in 396 CE, years after the Roman Empire had been converted to the religion of Jesus. As Jacob says, that was the date the new bread-god fully arrived.

Still, because the people continued to love her, the Roman Catholic Church allowed – but never made official – a Saint Demetra, patroness of grain, who was honoured joyfully for centuries.

We might wonder from this if religion is simply fashioned out of elements that have gone before, a quilt assembled for our comfort from scraps of clothing from long-dead relatives. Perhaps that's true. Perhaps religions grow out of one another, as trees grow out of an old trunk, absorbing nourishment as the old one fades to earth.

But that is part of their beauty. The bread-god Jesus, to my mind, is just made stronger by the lovely history of a thousand years that went before him. I treasure bread – buying it or making it or taking a ceremonious bite in church – for both these strong deities. Bread speaks to me of love, which is what Jesus commanded and what Demeter displayed.

It reminds me of my aunts, sitting with their first-prize-winning baker mother around a dining table in Northern Ontario. Years later, when all the daughters were married and living away from her, we took my grandmother to the airport to pick up one of my aunts who was by then living in Vancouver. My aunt flew off the plane as if she had wings herself. Their mutual expression of three-dimensional joy remains in my memory even now.

Bread makes me think of my grandmother and of my daughter – and of my mother, too, despite her conviction (now dispelled) that store-bought, white sliced bread marked the pinnacle of history. We are all made richer by the story of a love between a mother and a daughter that's so strong it stops the world.

BREAD AS GIFT, NOT ENEMY

The mythic power of bread makes those times when we withhold it from ourselves in the name of beauty all the more strange. There is no life without desire. Constant over-indulgence is another story, I believe, of a hunger for something other than bread: self-worth, self-love, dignity.

Perhaps our fear of carbohydrates comes from having them so easily available. A visiting Kenyan friend – who had earlier hosted me and another woman in her village – reached out her arms to me on arrival in Toronto and shouted, "My sister, you're so fat!" I did my best imitation of a tranquil face, but Alice could see she had made a social error and was sincerely puzzled. It is a compliment, in the village of Dumbeni, to be considered fat. Nobody is.

The women of rural Kenya carry water in 20-litre buckets on their heads for long distances. They walk for miles to gather firewood. They hoe and plant and weed and look after children and bend at the waist to wash dishes in basins on the ground. When all that is done, they make *ugali*, which is maize pounded into flour and cooked and stirred over an open fire until it is so firm you can slice it. The women made thick, tough, delicious chicken stew in our honour in Dumbeni, and we dipped it up with chunks of *ugali* and found that nothing had ever tasted better in the world.

Eating food – such as *ugali*, the bread of Kenya – that friends have made for you is a humbling pleasure. Perhaps they would say the making made them happy too. That's how it seemed, at least – a great and generous pleasure that they were glad to share.

When many of us women in North America have the luxury of living deeply in our heads, tapping computer keys for a living, the taste of fresh bread gives balance to our lives. When we make it ourselves, we begin to understand that it is very precious. Once in a while, we could simply allow the wisdom of our hands to push and pull the dough until the mind is rested, and the body is tired from generous work that others will enjoy.

A Simple Whole Wheat Loaf

Whole wheat flour has lots of gluten in it (the protein that helps make the dough elastic), but it takes a little longer to rise than white flour. It also has more wheat germ oil, so it should be stored in a cool place and used within a few months, if possible. The flavour in this loaf is well worth the little bit of extra effort.

1 tbsp. (15 mL) yeast

2½ cups (625 mL) warm water

3 tbsp. (45 mL) honey

2½ tsp. (12 mL) salt

3 tbsp. (45 mL) butter, melted

6–7 cups (1.5–1.75 L) whole wheat flour

Combine yeast and water in a large bowl. Stir in honey, salt, and butter. Whisk in 2 cups of the flour, cover, and set aside in a warm place (on top of the kitchen sink filled with hot or warm water, or near a fireplace does nicely) until it has bubbled up into a "sponge," about an hour.

Beat the mixture, folding in 2 more cups of flour, one cup at a time. Flour the clean counter well, and turn the mixture out onto it. Flour your hands well, too, and knead for about 15 minutes, pausing to put more flour on your hands and the counter. (For those unaccustomed to sticky fingers, have patience. This dough stays sticky for a long time, and will never be quite as smooth as the white.)

Wash the bowl, dry and oil it, and put your ball of dough into it, turning it to coat it with oil. Cover with a clean tea towel and let rise in that same warm place until double, about 1½ to 2 hours.

Punch down and let rise again, about an hour.

Divide in two, shape into loaves, place into two oiled bread pans, and let rise again in the same warm place, about 20 minutes.

Bake in a preheated 350°F (175°C) oven for about 40 to 50 minutes, and turn out onto a rack to cool.

5
Bread as Welcome

It's important to have traditions around Christmas. I know that. Sometimes, though, tradition overwhelms. The tea rings, for instance. I always make tea rings at Christmas, four or even eight at a time. They are decadent and quite lovely large round rings cut cunningly with scissors and twisted to resemble cinnamon-and-raisin-laden buttery wreaths. These are baked and then (gilding the lily) spread with white icing, sprinkled with chopped pecans, and made seasonal with red and green cherry halves.

Yes, it's over the top. But it's Christmas, when we celebrate the extravagant love of God, and feast to get us through the longest days of winter.

This season is about hospitality and warmth, companionship and firelight. It is the season of Hestia, goddess of the hearth; and of Mary, the young mother for whom the humblest stable becomes a home that welcomes kings.

At one point Christmas came pretty close to killing me.

Some other women might say the same. The thing is, I was good at making this bread, and I made more and more: bread for the bazaar, bread for the neighbours, bread for the parties at our

If the divine creator has taken pains to give us delicious and exquisite things to eat, the least we can do is prepare them well and serve them with ceremony.

– FERNAND POINT (1897-1955)

99

house. I was – am – extremely proud of this bread. Seldom have I felt more virtuous as when carrying my still-warm, fragrant circles into the church bake sale and hearing sighs of admiration.

Other traditions – the fresh green tree, the New Year's brunch – gave way to absent children, a busy job, a spouse living in another city, travel. But not the bread. Then one Christmas, exhausted, I pushed the large bowl into the oven to keep it warm, forgot about it, and later turned the oven on. I was making bread in two large metal bowls, which allowed me to up my production by having a second huge batch ready as the first was done.

Somehow I always forgot to factor into my planning the fact that I was going to have to stay awake until all eight rings were baked, two at a time. (In fact, I had begun to yearn for a household version of Britain's 1954 Night Baking Act, which had ended the practice of bakery employees staying up all night to produce bread for the morning.)

Soon I smelled hot bread and realized what I had done. I blearily rushed to the kitchen to rescue the dough. Too late. It had already formed a crust and – with the mixture for four big tea rings in one metal bowl-turned-hot-pan – looked to be on the way to becoming the largest loaf my kitchen had ever produced.

But I was too exhausted to worry. I hurled the dough onto the counter and shaped it into simple loaves instead of the usual elaborate rings, hustled it into quickly-oiled loaf pans, let it rise, and threw it back in the oven.

The bread that resulted was miraculous. It sliced neatly and slid into the toaster without choking it with icing. We had toast instead of tea rings that Christmas. Tradition was broken. The world did not come to an end.

I still make tea rings at Christmas. If any grown children are home, they assist, making it psychologically much easier for them to take one along when visiting a friend. I love their companionship. And I still love the richness of the dough and the sense of my own virtue at the sight of buttery wreaths on the dining table, ready to be given to people I cherish.

But I have learned that I am not immortal. I have slid down from a mountainous bread-baking ego trip and discovered that my friends still love me, and will come to visit whether I make tea rings or not.

Welcome Home

There are some clues here about tradition, which is meant to serve us and to contain our memories, not the other way around. In the same way, hospitality is meant to rest, not overwhelm, a guest. Simple is fine, as in the stories of welcome below.

Hestia's Hearth Fire

Hestia, sister to Zeus and Demeter, rules the hearth fire, the quiet centre of the household. Hence her importance at Christmas, the essentially hospitable time of year.

Hestia was the first-born of the Titan Cronus, who was so threatened by his children that he swallowed them whole. When Zeus and Gaia (Mother Earth) forced Cronus to spit up his now-grown children, a war ensued in heaven, which consumed the gods until they took up residence on Mount Olympus. But (according to some versions of the story) Hestia gave up her status to live among humans and to teach them to build houses.

She never married (perhaps affected by her bizarre childhood) but, as author and analyst Jean Shinoda Bolen reports in *Goddesses in Older Women: Archetypes in Women Over Fifty*, remains "one-in-herself," a virgin goddess.

Bolen explains that "Hestia is an inwardly focused consciousness needed for contemplation and prayer." She is able "to intuitively sense the essence of a situation or the character of a person. She has a natural detachment, and seeks tranquility."

The first of every sacrifice to the gods belonged to the tranquil Hestia. In Roman times, emigrating colonists took her fire for their new homes; and when a daughter married, her mother ceremoniously brought fire from the family hearth. Just as Demeter was the beloved goddess of the farmer, Hestia was the primary goddess of the baker, for without her hearth fire there would be no bread.

There would have to be bread, some rich, whole-grain bread and zwieback, and perhaps on a long, narrow dish some pale Westphalian ham laced with strips of white fat like an evening sky with bands of clouds. There would be some tea ready to be drunk, yellowish golden tea in glasses with silver saucers, giving off a faint fragrance.

~ RAINER MARIA RILKE
(1875-1926)

The Widow's Meal

Back to Elijah, surviving in the wilderness until drought drives him from the wadi. God whispers to him again, perhaps in a dream. "Elijah, you should start hiking," says God (or words to that effect), "and now you will be fed by a widow in a town called Zarephath."

Elijah stands exhausted in front of the town gate, feeling lost and very thirsty. He approaches a woman balancing her water jar and a collection of thin firewood. "Bring me a little water," he pleads, and – pressing his luck as she readies the jar – shouts, "Oh, and a morsel of bread in your other hand."

The woman turns and is very direct. "As the Lord your God lives," she snaps, "I have no bread baked, only a little flour and little oil, but I am going to build a fire and prepare some for myself and my son." Then, she says, "I and my son will eat it and die."

It wasn't a great welcome. But, to be fair, it was a very bad drought. King Ahab had been wicked, and the king is responsible for the whole land. If he isn't in proper friendship with God, everyone suffers. The woman has enough meal for one flat cake.

But by now Elijah has deduced she is the widow God has in mind. He tells her to make three cakes, first a little one for him, and then two more for her and her son. Her jar of flour will not be emptied, he tells her, and the jug of oil will not run dry "until the day God sends the rain upon the earth." For three long years, Elijah enjoys her initially unwilling hospitality. It never rains. But there is always just enough oil and meal for bread.

When we cast our bread upon the waters, we can presume that someone downstream whose face we will never know will benefit from our action, as we who are downstream from another will profit from that grantor's gift.

– Maya Angelou

Mary's Boy Child

Mary's essential hospitality as the obedient bearer of a child she has not sought is obvious when the angel Gabriel announces that she has "found favour with God." Mary points out that she is a virgin, and that this pregnancy is impossible. Gabriel says that not only will her child be the Son of God, but that her cousin Elizabeth, said to be barren, has also conceived a child.

Mary figuratively throws up her hands. "Let it be with me according to your word."

The Christmas story then moves to the practical hospitality of the keeper of the already overflowing inn, who sees Mary's swollen belly and provides a place in the stable. Here the newest god-child, hero of a thousand children's stories, is delivered, swaddled, and laid in a manger. He is welcomed by creatures of the barn, and shepherds lured by singing angels. Wise men arrive like long-lost aunties bearing gifts, kneeling in the dung to admire and coo.

It's a humble, if exuberant, beginning to a life. This infant will grow up as human as the shepherds and the wise men. Someday he will sit down with his friends, break open a loaf of bread, and ask them to imagine a world where there is more than enough bread for all.

The Bread of Welcome

I pull out the bin of flour and rescue the yeast from the back of the cupboard. Sometimes this is the first real bread baking after summer, even though it is late now, close to Christmas. I am in need of the imperturbability of Hestia and Mary.

They knew that true hospitality is a kind of quiet. Says Bolen, "Hestia... [has] an emotional warmth that is generous and not possessive... she does not polarize anyone because she is at home in the quiet in herself. In her presence... other people can also just be."

"Just being" may be why we are drawn to those familiar pageant images: barnyard beasts and kings, smelly shepherds and angels, the mother of God and her baby, all curiously at ease. "Tending to household tasks is a centring activity," says Bolen. "With Hestia there is no rush, no eye on the clock nor any internal critic. What she does pleases her and absorbs her."

That's what making bread does. It pleases and absorbs and centres us, making us better hosts not because we have something symbolic and delicious at hand, although we do, but because we are at peace. Unrushed, in the busiest season of the year. It is hospitality that welcomes a troubled friend, soothes a student far from home, and offers advice only when asked.

Of course, there's that candid widow greeting Elijah with the news that she and her son will have their one last bite before starvation claims them. Her reflexive, if cranky, hospitality saves her. She feeds him first, one small cake for the guest. There will be enough, he says. And there is.

True hospitality knows there will be enough. We're not good at that in our shiny, capitalist century. "You let a lot of children go to school hungry," Elijah the prophet whispers to us. (Prophets, you understand, don't tell the future. They tell the present.) "In the richest country in the world, you suggest there is not enough to go around."

I hope Elijah will be heard. I keep all their voices in my heart: Hestia, Mary, the widow-woman; and the baby bread-god, Jesus, saying what others have said before. Make your bread and take pleasure in the making of it. Give it away. Gather it up and feed five thousand. Or cast it upon the waters like a child feeding ducks. Best, sit around a common table and eat and talk together. There is enough. No one should be hungry while anyone has bread.

In my warm and sleepy kitchen, I shout for the nearest offspring to come and oil the pans, as my mother did for my grandmother.

CHRISTMAS TEA RINGS

1 cup (250 mL) white sugar

1 cup (250 mL) warm water (not hot)

4 tbsp. (60 mL) active dry yeast

14–15 cups (3.5–3.75 L)

    unbleached all-purpose flour

3 cups (750 mL) lukewarm milk

4 tsp. (20 mL) salt

4 eggs

1 cup (250 mL) soft butter

For each ring:

½ cup (125 mL) brown sugar

½ cup (125 mL) raisins

2 tsp. (10 mL) cinnamon (Be generous. Add more if you like.)

2 tbsp. (30 mL) butter

2 tbsp. (30 mL) chopped nuts (pecans or walnuts)

6 or more maraschino cherries (red and green) sliced in half

White icing:

1 cup (250 mL) icing sugar

1 tsp. (5 mL) vanilla

approx. 2 tbsp. (30 mL) milk

    (just enough to moisten to spreading consistency)

In large bowl, mix white sugar into water. Add yeast and let sit about 5 minutes until mixture is bubbly. Add milk, salt, eggs, butter, and half of the flour to the yeast mixture. Mix until smooth.

Add enough remaining flour to handle easily. Turn onto a floured board and knead until smooth, 8 to 10 minutes.

Round up in greased bowl; bring greased side up. Cover with cloth. Let rise in warm place until double, about 1½ hours. If kitchen is cool, place bowl on a rack over hot water, and cover completely with a towel.

Punch down. Let rise again until almost double, about 30 minutes. Shape as follows: Divide dough into four pieces. Roll out each piece into an oblong; spread it with butter, then sprinkle with brown sugar, about ½ cup for an oblong about 9x15 inches (22x38 cm). Sprinkle generously with cinnamon, then with ½ cup (125 mL) raisins. Roll up tightly, beginning at the wide side, and seal the edge by pinching it together. Place sealed-edge down in a ring on a lightly greased baking sheet. Pinch ends together to make a circle.

With scissors, make cuts ⅔ of the way through the ring, at 1-inch intervals. Turn each of these sections on their side. (Be firm; bread dough can take it.)

Let rise until double.
Bake at 375°F (190°C) for
25 to 30 minutes. (Check
to make sure it doesn't
get too brown.) While still
warm, frost with a simple
white icing and decorate
with nuts and cherries.
Serve warm, or wrap in
foil and freeze, reheating
later in the same foil.

White icing

Mix icing sugar, vanilla,
and milk in a small bowl.
It may be a bit thick, but
it will soften on the warm
bread dough, holding the
nuts in place; and then it
firms nicely.

Hints

1. The secret to successful bread dough is to remember that it is alive. If it gets too cold, it goes into hibernation. If it gets too hot, it dies.

2. Warm the flour in 200°F (95°C) oven before adding it as a way of speeding up the rising.

3. Heat the milk in the microwave, and then add the butter to it, so it is warm as well.

4. You can cut this recipe in half, or even one-fourth, although making just one always seems to me like a waste of energy by the time you've sorted out the ingredients.

5. Finally, now that it is the 21st century, it is okay to use instant or fast-rising yeast. I guess. In that case, first mix the dry yeast into the other dry ingredients, and have the water and milk much warmer before you add them all at once, along with the eggs and butter. It rises much faster, and as far as I can tell, makes no difference to the quality of the dough.

6
Bread as Peace

The best tortillas I ever tasted were made from fresh ground cornmeal in El Salvador two decades ago. Social activists were in and out of every Central American country then, trying to ease the civil conflicts sweeping through like brush fires, hurting the poor most of all.

My husband, Jim, was the first of our family to visit the people of the corn, the *campesinos* of Central America. When he came back, he was full of stories. He told, for example, how in San Dionisio, Nicaragua, a rooster crows at first light, and hens begin to call their chicks from under a visitor's cot. Then, Nora, the mother of this household, begins to move around, and a couple of children are handed a basin of corn kernels to take to the small electric mill owned jointly by the villagers.

This village has electricity, but its effect on individual homes is only to provide for one bare light bulb, hanging from the rafters. Cooking is done on an open fire built directly on a concrete counter, with smoke rising gently to the roof and seeping out through gaps left for that purpose between the bricks.

Later, he returned to visit Mayan villages overlooking Lake Atitlán, where women walked eight miles to a mill to grind their

corn. (The church he was representing later provided money for a communal mill, so they could grind it in their own village.)

It is hard to imagine corn as a weapon. But that's what it was in Central America in the 1980s. From his impassioned accounts, I began to understand how impossible it is to overstate the importance of corn to *campesinos*, and how vulnerable that dependency makes them. Everyone in the villages depends on the corn. It is their hope, their food, their way of life, their religion. This is where corn began. Over thousands of years, the ancestors of these people had slowly produced larger and larger cobs from *teosinte*, a perennial grass.

But the *campesinos* had been driven off their land and away from their crops by the rich landowners in power, who sent soldiers in helicopter gunships to spray the fields with bullets. Human rights organizations and churches in North America, appalled by the death toll, tried to influence their own governments in favour of the peasants. In Canada, that meant arguing for the federal government to stand up against our U.S. ally, who was supporting the Salvadoran regime to the tune of over a million dollars a day.

When I went myself in 1989 – one of a trio of church representatives – people weary of life in refugee camps were struggling to return home. Their children, they said, were forgetting how to plant the corn.

We were taken into the countryside to visit a *campesino* we knew only as José. As the head of an agricultural cooperative, he was in grave danger from those who feared the words "co-op" and "union," because what those words represent threatened their stranglehold on the nation's economy.

A few weeks before our visit, soldiers had taken our host from his house and tied him to a tree. They had put a grenade in his mouth and taunted him, saying, "We are going to kill you, old man." His wary, sullen 20-year-old neighbour told us how he had been beaten by soldiers, who told him to get up and run or they would shoot him.

We met a young woman, visibly pregnant, turning gleaming white corn that was drying in the sunlight, almost ready for milling. Her husband had been taken away by soldiers and was being held in a nearby military barracks. José showed us the cooperative's fields of pineapple and okra, dangerously weedy. So many men had fled in fear, there was no one left to care for them.

Finally, we were seated around a table on the hard-packed earth, which formed both José's yard and the floor of his house, and were served delicious stacks of hot tortillas with rice and beans.

It may seem strange that any men should dare to ask a just God's assistance in wringing their bread from the sweat of other men's faces.

~ ABRAHAM LINCOLN

Many years later, the taste of those tortillas is as fresh as it was then. So is my awe at their makers' courage. You see, after we had eaten, we climbed into our van to return to the city. José jumped in with us. He and the other members of the cooperative's council were going to the barracks to demand the release of the young man whose wife looked after the shining corn they hoped their child would learn to grow.

JOHN SULLIVAN AND
THE DESTRUCTION OF THE CORN

Bread has been used as a weapon throughout history. Closer to my own home in Ontario – but more than two centuries earlier – corn was a player in the American Revolution. When the Six Nations of the Iroquois Confederacy split in their allegiance, with two of them siding with the rebel Americans and four (most of the Mohawks, Cayugas, Onondagas, and Senecas) with the British, reprisal against the Loyalists was terribly harsh.

After several furious battles and accusations (which may or may not have been true) of non-combatant deaths against the Iroquois, Commander George Washington gave orders for "the total destruction and devastation of their settlements, and the capture of as many prisoners of every age and sex as possible. It will be essential to ruin their crops now in the ground and prevent their planting more… that the country may not be merely overrun, but destroyed."

In an eerie foretaste of the *campesinos'* troubles two centuries later, Washington further ordered that there must be no peace without the "complete ruination" of the Iroquois settlements. "Our future security will be… in the terror with which the chastisement they receive will inspire them."

And so it was. General John Sullivan wrote in his journal in 1779 that "the quantity of corn destroyed… must amount to

160,000 bushels… I flatter myself that the orders with which I was entrusted are fully executed, as we have not left a single settlement or field of corn in the country of the Five Nations."

Bread Battles

It is unforgivable to use food as a weapon in battle, but disputes involving bread are hardly new. Dreadful conditions existed for European peasants in the Middle Ages, for instance. They grew the grain, but lost much of their own harvest to the landowner. They had to pay the miller to grind what little grain they had. The miller himself, though, was also a tenant and had to pay his own rent to the lord of the manor. So the miller – to survive – had to steal some of the grain the peasant brought for milling. And because he was valuable "among the technically ignorant men of the Middle Ages," as H. K. Jacob explains, a technician who knew how to run the complicated water mill, the miller was not easy to get rid of in spite of his sins. Witness Chaucer's *The Miller's Tale*, with its portrait of the thieving miller and the bawdy tale of revenge undertaken by two hungry students.

Through the ages, bread has been subsidized, regulated, deregulated. It has been infested with vermin and contaminated with sand by millers seeking to disguise their theft. It has been supplemented with lashings of alum, potato-starch, and bone ash (bakers during Britain's industrial revolution were accused, rightly or wrongly, of worse).

Perhaps most horrifying, rye flour in the troubled Middle Ages sometimes harboured the fungus *claviceps purpurea*, which in turn produces ergotoxine, an alkaloid similar to LSD. Made into bread, it drove those who consumed it mad. In 943 CE, Jacob relates, "shrieking, wailing, and writhing men collapsed in the street. Many stood up from their tables and rolled like wheels through the room; others toppled over and foamed in epileptic convulsions; still others vomited …and screamed, "Fire! I'm burning!"

Forty thousand people died in Europe in a single year – mainly because of a lack of learning in "the arts of tilling and baking" that the Romans knew so well, says Jacob.

Much later, when Hitler's armies invaded Europe, hunger became a weapon again, a "*pact de famine*" Jacob calls it, "to alter the population figures of Europe for the benefit of Germany." Jacob himself ate a mixture of sawdust, potato flour and peas in Buchenwald, where he was interned, and where "many died without ever tasting real bread again."

Today, grains in North America, home of the breadbasket of the world, are rich and plentiful, and subject to completely differ- ent pressures. The family farm is frequently forced to the margins as industrialized agriculture – which controls seeds, fertilizers, pesticides, machinery, and often markets – creates larger and larger acreages. Marketing agencies protecting the farmer, such as the huge and elderly Canadian Wheat Board, come under fire from free trade agreements. (This battle may be speeded along by a federal government sympathetic to free trade. In early October 2006, the Conservative government ordered the Wheat Board's governors not to spend money on advertising, publishing, or any market research that would help them argue for its retention.)

In the face of unjust burdens on small farmers, consumers can help. We can shop at farmers' markets. In some communities, we can buy shares ahead of time in a season's crop, spreading the risk for the farmer. And we can shop at bakeries such as the warm-hearted Ace Bakery, in Toronto, which supports local food programs.

There's no bigger success story in the warm-heart category, though, than the Tall Grass Prairie Bread Company. It's a bakery at the Forks, a busy Winnipeg shopping area, to which a friend proudly led me during a visit to her city. Marvellous aromas filled the place, along with a crowd of people buying cinnamon buns and bread.

It seemed like any other bakery, though, until my friend told its story. The bakery had begun as a cooperative venture by a group of church people and their neighbours who wanted to reduce the gap between farmer and customer. Farmers were getting the short end of the loaf, so to speak, as a result of low grain prices, and the group thought they could help by buying wheat directly from the producer. They could afford to pay a bit more for it, if they milled it themselves and baked it together as a co-op.

That went well. As members set out to help more farmers, the co-op grew into a full-fledged bakery, which now has two outlets

Bakers of bread rolls and pastry cooks will not buy grain before eleven o'clock in winter and noon in summer; bakers of large loaves will not buy grain before two o'clock. This will enable the people of the town to obtain their supply first. Bakers shall put a distinctive trademark on their loaves, and keep weights and scales in their shops, under penalty of having their licences removed.

~ 1635 Law Introduced by Cardinal Richelieu

(the Forks is the second), employs about four dozen Winnipeggers, and makes many more very happy. The place is crowded because the bread is terrific, with assorted fascinating loaves all made from grain that is delivered from local farms. And all of it organic.

By this time, I was trying to figure out how many loaves I could squeeze into my suitcase for the trip home.

We are blessed with abundant food on this continent. Whether or not we bake it ourselves, we have an array of choices. The flour we buy can be stone-ground, unbleached, whole wheat, or organic; our bread can be augmented with the likes of soya flour, barley flakes, cornmeal, bulgar, or bran.

This abundance implies a responsibility to be fair to those who grow the grain. Most of us can afford to pay a fair price for good bread. And in a shrinking world, where we can buy quinoa and spelt almost as easily as wheat flour, we need to look to the welfare of small farmers in other countries as well, by questioning trade deals that favour industrialization.

It doesn't all rest on the consumer. Despite the pressure towards bigger farming, organizations such as the National Farmers' Union and Seeds of Diversity Canada aim to preserve family farms, and heritage seeds, respectively. Somewhere inside us, the idea remains that our grains are as holy as the Mayan *campesinos'* corn.

Slow Food

Bread needs to be handled with care. It connects us with the history of the world and – more importantly – our own history. A friend describes her young son coming home from school one Friday afternoon to find the challah loaves ready for Shabbat. "Oh Mommy," he said happily, "you're making memories."

For less than the cost of a Big Mac, fries and a Coke, you can buy a loaf of fresh bread and some good cheese or roast beef, which you will enjoy much more.

~ STEVE ALBINI

With an eye to future memories, it's worth considering how we eat the food we receive. A nation where friends or families lack time to gather around a common table – a fast food nation, as Eric Schlosser points out in his book of that name – damages our bodies, our local economies, and our souls.

Bread is the ultimate slow food. It takes all day. We need slow. Food needs to be eaten with as much leisure as we can find. This is not to keep women barefoot in the kitchen, especially when men can cook. It is to savour precious things like conversation and the stories of the day.

If the divine creator has taken pains to give us delicious and exquisite things to eat, the least we can do is prepare them well and serve them with ceremony.

~ FERNAND POINT (1897–1955)

132

The slowness of bread calls us to simple meals, local food if possible, seasonal vegetables. It's terribly hard to do this, of course, in a culture that makes efficiency a god and two incomes a necessity. And I have no real knowledge, no real advice to give. When our children were young, our own family meals were, too often, frantically torn out of an already stretched daily fabric.

But happy meals that have nothing to do with a quick burger and everything to do with attentive ears and simple food – grown and marketed justly – are worth seeking despite the odds. Grown children remember them. Anything that is so full of meaning as bread needs to be handled slowly and with love.

Cooking is at once one of the simplest and most gratifying of the arts, but to cook well one must love and respect food.

– CRAIG CLAIBORNE

All well-regulated families set apart an hour every morning for tea and bread and butter.

– JOSEPH ADDISON (1672–1719)

A Somewhat Global Bread

I make this bread when I become overwhelmed with the idea that I am responsible for the health of those I love. Mostly, they live too far away and are way too grown-up for me to put into practice this slightly unbalanced view of the world. But when they are expected home, I deal with my excitement by making quantities of soup and a hoard of this bread. Dinner is never a problem.

2 tbsp. (30 mL) dry yeast (traditional, not instant)

6 cups (1.5 L) warm water

4 tbsp. (60 mL) honey

4 tbsp. (60 mL) molasses

4 cups (1 L) unbleached white flour

8 cups (approx.) (2 L) whole wheat flour

½ cup (125 mL) canola oil

2 tbsp. (30 mL) salt

1½ cups (375 mL) rolled oats

1½ cups (375 mL) quinoa or barley flakes

1½ cups (375 mL) bulgar or cornmeal

1 cup (250 mL) rye flour

1 cup (250 mL) oat bran

1 egg (beaten with a little water)

Sesame or poppy seeds, or rolled oats

Dissolve yeast in water in a very large bowl and add honey and molasses. Let sit for a few minutes until it is foamy. Gradually whisk in the unbleached white flour and 4 cups (1 L) of the whole wheat flour, then beat well with a wooden spoon. Cover with a tea towel and leave in a warm place until spongy, about an hour.

Mix in the oil and salt, then add all the grains, oat bran and flours except the remaining whole wheat, one after another, mixing after each addition. Then add 2 cups of the remaining whole wheat flour and turn the whole thing out onto a very well floured clean counter and knead for 15 minutes, adding more flour as necessary.

You will find this much heavier than the white dough you made earlier. Do not despair. Keep kneading. This ball of dough will never be as smooth as a simple white dough, but it will eventually hold its shape. Let it sit while you wash and oil the big bowl. Put the dough into it and turn so the oiled side is up. Cover with a tea towel and put it back in the warm spot until double, about an hour. (Placing it on an oven rack placed over a sink full of very hot water is good, especially if you don't need the sink for a while.)

Put the bowl on the counter and punch down (you might take this opportunity to refill the sink with hot water), then put back in the warm place, and leave it for another hour.

Butter four loaf pans. Use lots of butter. (If you like, you can line the pans with parchment paper instead, which is more labour-intensive but guarantees an easy exit from the pan after baking.) With a sharp knife, cut the risen dough into four parts. Shape each part into a loaf and place in a pan.

Brush the tops with egg mixture and sprinkle with seeds or oatmeal. Let rise to the tops of the pans. Bake in a preheated 350°F (175°C) oven on the middle rack for about an hour, until the bread sounds hollow when you tap the top. Brush once, at about 30 minutes, with the egg mixture.

Take out of the pans, using a sharp knife if necessary, and cool, propped up or on a rack.

* This freezes nicely, but don't thaw it in a microwave or it will be tough. You can halve the recipe, but getting all those grains out of the cupboard seems onerous unless you are making a big batch. With quinoa, this is a very crunchy loaf, which we like. But you may wish to try barley flakes instead.

Bread that must be sliced with an axe is bread that is too nourishing.

~ FRAN LEBOWITZ

7

Bread for Body and Soul

Once, on retreat at the monastery of St. Benoit du Lac in Quebec's Eastern Townships, our little group was invited to participate in the Eucharist with the monks. I lined up with the others, touched by the chanting of the choir and the unfamiliar scent of incense. Suddenly, just before I was to receive the bread, I became extremely dizzy and had to lie down on the floor for a while.

This created some stir. The Roman Catholics in the room seemed poised to believe I was having a religious experience. My Protestant friends, with whom I was making this retreat, were more inclined to remember that on occasions of religious ceremony I am subject to losing consciousness, and that Communion is a particularly dangerous time.

I have no idea why this happens. Perhaps it is simply the introvert's exceeding self-consciousness, wondering how this mere mortal dares approach God – even ritually. Or perhaps it is an awareness at a deep level that this symbolic act of eating bread and drinking wine forms a powerful nexus of many times and cultures, a kind of ley line of the spirit.

I wish this tendency would go away. However, since it has been part of me for nearly all my life and seems unlikely to disappear, I will settle for simply figuring out what this strange – but clearly powerful – act of sharing bread and wine might mean.

Even within that lovely monastery chapel, there would have been a difference of opinion about the nature of the bread on offer. Traditional Catholic teaching would say it was the actual body of Jesus, transformed by the ritual. I and the other Protestants were content to believe it was a symbolic act of great importance and solemnity – except, of course, for my comical inability to remain vertical.

Sacred Bread as Memory

Those two opinions alone are confusing enough. But add in the parallels with the ritual of the grain goddess, Demeter, when her people made their pilgrimage accompanied by Bacchus, the god of wine. It's true that "the millions of people who were initiated in Eleusis between the seventh century BCE and the fourth century CE all kept their vows of silence," as H. K. Jacob says, in his book *Six Thousands Years of Bread*. But we do know some significant details.

"Eleusis meant 'advent,'" says Barbara G. Walker, in *The Woman's Encyclopedia of Myths and Secrets*. "Its principal rites brought about the advent of the Divine Child or Savior...like corn, he was born of Demeter-the-earth and laid in a manger or winnowing basket. His flesh was eaten by communicants in the form of bread, made from the first or last sheaves. His blood was drunk in the form of wine. Like Jesus, he entered the earth and rose again. Communicants were supposed to partake of his immortality..."

A look at Isis, the Egyptian goddess of almost everything, including bread, only adds to our bewilderment. Her son Horus, for example, is referred to by author Tom Harpur as "the pagan Christ," in his book of that name. Harper explores many parallels between Jesus and Horus: his birth heralded by a star, his baptism, his walking on water, his crucifixion, his descent into Hell, his resurrection, and his self-awareness as the "bread of life."

"Horus declared, in the Egyptian ritual, I am the possessor of bread in Anu. I have bread in heaven with Ra," Harpur explains. He goes on to explain how the principle of wisdom and compassion and healing, which some call Christ, can't be confined to any one faith, can't "bid all the world to come to it – on its terms alone." It already exists in each person, "the divinity in every single human being."

Bread deals with living things, with giving life, with growth, with the seed, the grain that nurtures. It's not coincidence that we say bread is the staff of life.

– LIONEL POILNE

Perhaps the taste of a tiny morsel of bread in a heightened ceremonial setting simply overwhelms me with these ancient truths in narrative form, the archetypal knowledge I share with all humanity. Perhaps it calls up a bone-deep memory of a time when we humans lived firmly on one piece of land, and understood in a visceral way that if the crop fails, we die.

You can see why I get dizzy confronted by the bread and the wine.

Sacred Bread as Community

Jesus may have been lent significance by his association with other gods of bread. But that doesn't account for the power of his celebration, which persists daily around the world.

Everywhere, the words are similar: "He took a loaf of bread and after blessing it he broke it, gave it to them and said, 'Take, this is my body.'" And, everywhere, people line up, blue-jean clad or robed, young or old, to receive bits of bread; or they sit in pews and pass tiny chunks on a plate; or they stand in a circle and murmur a blessing as a broken loaf moves from hand to hand.

Sometimes they simply gather around a sickbed.

Once, I sat in a circle of friends, in a smoky cabin in the bush, after a weekend of tending a woodstove and talking about dreams. We passed the bread around as gently as if it were the heart of the other, which it was.

The ritual has power. I get uneasy if I think I might be left out. Once, reporting on an event, I slipped up to take a photo of Archbishop Desmond Tutu serving Communion, and then paused anxiously. He winked and held out the bread.

Perhaps inclusion is this ceremony's strength. This bread offers an enormous community, a family that stretches around the world and through the centuries. We don't want to be left out.

Love just doesn't sit there, like a stone, it has to be made, like bread; re-made all the time, made new.

– Ursula K. LeGuin

SACRED BREAD AS TRANSFORMATION

The power of the Eucharist may simply be that of all sacred drama: the promise of change. In the Eleusian Mysteries, for instance, the ritual transforms not the bread, but the initiates. As Karen Armstrong explains in *The Great Transformation: The Beginning of Our Religious Traditions*, "the *mystai* did not go to Eleusis to learn anything, but to have an experience that they felt transformed them. 'I came out of the mystery hall,' one of the *mystai* recalled, 'feeling a stranger to myself.'"

In the same deep way as the trek to Eleusis changed the ancient Greeks, the re-enactment of Jesus' last conversation with his friends says that those who share a meal with the compassionate one can become just and brave agents of healing. Such bread offers the hope of human change.

That's why, over and over, I form a circle with my friends and say the words, "The bread of new life…"

Bread and Sacrifice

The celebration of Communion is also a powerful experience of metaphor. Bread as body. Wine as blood. Love as sacrifice.

In the Jesus story, it is clear that love has great requirements. There is a price to pay, in an oppressive era, for feeding the unwanted.

It may help to see another story, that of the Celtic Earth goddess Tailtiu, queen of the Fir Bolg, one of the ancient peoples of pre-Christian Ireland.

When Tailtiu saw that her people were starving after an insufficient grain harvest, she took up an axe and, for a solid year, cleared a forest: "the reclaiming of meadowland from even wood by Tailtiu, daughter of Magmor," is the way it is reported by the anonymous bard of *The Dindsenchas,* poems about Irish place names.

After the trees had been cut down, "roots and all, out of the ground," the land became "a plain blossoming with clover," presumably suitable for planting grain. But the cost was appalling. Tailtiu's heart "burst in her body from the strain beneath her royal vest," the bard says. The Celts loved their sacred groves, and the destruction to the enchanted richness of her forest must have broken Tailtiu's heart.

Aware that she is dying, her courtiers gather around, and Tailtiu whispers her last command. She wants funeral games to be held in her honour each year, just before the harvest. And they are to be peaceful, she says, "without sin, without fraud, without reproach, without insult, without contention, without seizure, without theft."

Thanks to her faithful foster-child Lugh (later associated with a bountiful harvest), Tailtiu's wish came to pass. There was always an "unbroken truce" at her fair, and "men went in and came out without any rude hostility. Corn and milk in every stead, peace and fair weather for its sake, were granted to the heathen tribes of the Greeks for maintaining of justice."

The Peaceable Queendom

Tailtiu had given up her beloved forest and her life for a vision not too different from that of Archbishop Oscar Romero or of Mondawmin, who brought corn to the Ojibway. "Unbroken truce" and "corn and milk in every stead" represent the commonwealth of peace, the kingdom Jesus told his friends was close by. New parents get a glimpse of this kingdom looking at their tiny baby. Their sudden understanding that they would do anything to keep this child safe is the closest we can come, perhaps, to understanding the sacrifice that is part of love's potential.

Perhaps that's the power of Communion bread. Some say that it commemorates Jesus offering himself as a sacrifice for our sins, but I don't think so. I would be appalled by a god who asked for the death of his child, or any child. But like any parent, I believe I would die for my children's lives, even as absurdly grown-up as they are now.

Perhaps this bread simply expresses our wish to live a little closer to the ideal of Tailtiu, Jesus, or Mondawmin, who died to give their people enough to eat. None of us can stand up to greed or selfishness as strongly as we wish. But eating this ceremonial bread with others, who also want to be just and loving, makes us brave enough to try.

Maybe that's why I am sometimes overwhelmed at these ceremonies. Maybe I am simply terrified by the high sacrifices love assumes. Certainly the part most touching to me in the story of my own bread-god, Jesus, is not his death, but his constant focus on compassion. "Love one another as I have loved you," he commands. "Love your enemies."

Irish Soda Bread

On a cold rainy day, this bread (omit the raisins), served with a long-simmering stew for supper, is heaven. Or, if it is not a working day and you are at home in the afternoon, include the raisins and declare a day fit for an old-fashioned tea, with toasted slices of this bread, and cheese and marmalade.

1¾ cups (425 mL) buttermilk

1 egg

1 tsp. (5 mL) baking soda

3 tsp. (15 mL) baking powder

1¼ tsp. (6 mL) salt

2 cups (500 mL) unbleached white
    all-purpose flour

2 cups (500 mL) whole wheat flour

1 cup (250 mL) raisins (optional)

Preheat oven to 375°F (175°C). Mix dry ingredients in a large bowl, including raisins if you want them. Beat buttermilk and egg together and stir into the flour mixture. Turn out onto lightly floured board or clean counter and knead briefly, until smooth. Divide the dough in two, shape into flattened rounds, and place on baking sheet or into two greased cake tins. With a very sharp knife, slash an X across the tops. Bake 35 to 40 minutes.

Serve warm.

Conclusion

Bread as Meaning

According to an old Welsh legend, Christ went into a bakery and asked for some bread. The baker immediately put a piece of dough into the oven. But her daughter felt she was too generous, took it out, cut off half of it, and put it back in. It immediately grew into an enormous loaf, while the inhospitable daughter began to hoot with surprise. She had been turned into an owl (a practice reminiscent of Demeter, who was famous for changing those with whom she was annoyed into owls). One could draw from this any number of rules for life.

- ☙ If a stranger asks for bread, be generous.
- ☙ Be kind to stray owls. You don't know whose daughter they might be.
- ☙ Don't mess with bread that's already in the oven.
- ☙ Obey your mother at all times. Especially if she is a baker.
- ☙ Keep your door locked if you're too rude to share.

But my favourite possibility is this: Be alert, because the sacred might be at your door. Or perhaps it is found at a dinner table nearby, where friends gather and talk and make a doorway into a world where our souls are honoured.

As I was finishing this book, my friend Trisha, who sometimes worries that I will be found at my computer comatose from malnourishment, was hosting her usual Sunday evening gathering of six or seven friends, and invited me to join them. They offered helpful ideas. They discussed the way family history is passed down to children and grandchildren in conversation over shared tasks, such as making bread. They mused about the strengths of oral history, and the way putting words into print can close those histories down and set them in concrete. I told them how I'd broken old words apart in order to retell the story of Jesus' last supper with his friends; and how (to my surprise) it had come out happy, not solemn as it is in old paintings that hang on church walls.

They nodded understandingly. I came away happy and relieved, as if I had divine approval.

I think that's what the owl story is about. Holy moments may be found at any time. The peaceable kingdom is near, just over in the next dimension, where the banquet is ready, where there is always enough to go around, enough dear friends, enough sustaining conversation, enough approval. Enough bread.

This peaceful commonwealth can be found at dinner tables and picnics, birthday and anniversary celebrations in all their pleasure and sometimes panic, where – sometimes – the bread has been prepared by someone's flour-dusted hands in the way of our grandmothers.

The bread is only a *symbol* for love.

In a few weeks, my daughter will come to visit. Soon I will take down the bowl she gave me, and mix and stir. Here in my kitchen, fingers sticky with dough (and maybe someday, with young Elijah helping on a tall stool by my side), I will make my own meaning out of bread.

Let there be work, bread, water and salt for all.

~ Nelson Mandela

SOURCES

Books

Armstrong, Karen. *The Great Transformation: The Beginning of Our Religious Traditions.* New York: Knopf, 2006.

Bailey, Adrian. *The Blessings of Bread.* London: Paddington Press, 1975.

Betty Crocker editors. *Betty Crocker's New Picture Cook Book.* New York: McGraw-Hill, 1961.

Bolen, Jean Shinoda. *Goddesses in Older Women: Archetypes in Women Over Fifty.* New York: Quill, 2002.

Curry, Brother Rick, S. J. *The Secrets of Jesuit Breadmaking.* New York: HarperCollins, 1995.

Diamond, Jared. *Guns, Germs and Steel: The Fate of Human Societies.* New York: Norton, 1999.

Frye, Northrop. *The Educated Imagination.* Toronto: CBC Publications, 1963.

Fussell, Betty. *The Story of Corn.* New York: Knopf, 1992.

Harpur, Tom. *The Pagan Christ: Uncovering the Lost Light.* Toronto: Thomas Allen, 2005.

Heintzman, Andrew, and Evan Solomon. *Feeding the Future: From Fat to Famine, How to Solve the World's Food Crisis.* Toronto: Anansi, 2004.

Jacob, H. E. *Six Thousand Years of Bread: Its Holy and Unholy History.* New York: The Lyons Press, 1997. (Original publishers: Garden City: Doubleday, Doran and Company, 1944.)

King, R.H. and McKechnie. *Classical Mythology in Song and Story.* Toronto: Copp Clark, 1937.

King, Thomas. *The Truth about Stories: A Native Narrative.* Toronto: Anansi, 2003.

Kneen, Brewster. *From Land to Mouth: Understanding the Food System.* Toronto: NC Press, 1989.

Schlosser, Eric. *Fast Food Nation: The Dark Side of the American Meal.* New York: Houghton Mifflin, 2001.

Shulman, Martha Rose. *Great Breads: Home-Baked Favorites from Europe, the British Isles and North America*. Shelburne: Chapters, 1995.

The Holy Bible, New Revised Standard Version. Nashville: Thomas Nelson Publishers 1989.

Walker, Barbara G. *The Woman's Encyclopedia of Myths and Secrets*. New York: HarperSanFrancisco, 1983.

Wilson, Hap. *Canoeing, Kayaking and Hiking Temagami*. Erin: The Boston Mills Press, 2004.

Wright, Ronald. *A Short History of Progress*. Toronto: Anansi, 2004.

Websites

The Story behind a Loaf of Bread.
http://www.botham.co.uk/bread/index.htm

The Federation of Bakers.
http://www.bakersfederation.org.uk

Bread and Roses.
http://www.lucyparsonsproject.org/iww/kornbluh_bread_roses.html

Tailtiu.
http://www.ancienttexts.org/library/celtic/ctexts/d18.html

Demeter and Persephone.
http://www.stoa.org/diotima/anthology/demeter.shtml

Bake Ovens at Dufferin Grove Park.
http://www.dufferinpark.ca/oven/wiki/wiki.phpph

Photo credits